WHAT'S NEXT?
IRAN GOES NUCLEAR

**Connecting Today's Headlines to Tomorrow's
Prophetic Events**

JIMMY EVANS
MARK HITCHCOCK

WHAT'S NEXT?
IRAN GOES NUCLEAR

Connecting Today's Headlines to Tomorrow's
Prophetic Events

JIMMY EVANS
MARK HITCHCOCK

TIPPING POINT
— PRESS —

TIPPING POINT
— P R E S S —

What's Next? Iran Goes Nuclear: Connecting Today's Headlines to Tomorrow's Prophetic Events
Copyright © 2024 by Jimmy Evans and Mark Hitchcock

ISBN: 978-1-960870-41-4 Paperback
ISBN: 978-1-960870-42-1 eBook
ISBN: 979-8-89153-511-4 audiobook

Tipping Point Press creates resources to help people understand biblical
prophecy and the relevance of world events to the End Times. These
messages provide hope, peace, and encouragement. For more resources
visit EndTimes.com.

Tipping Point Press
1021 Grace Lane
Southlake, TX 76092

While the authors make every effort to provide accurate URLs at the time
of printing for external or third-party Internet websites, neither they nor
the publisher assume any responsibility for changes or errors made after
publication.

Printed in the United States of America

24 25 26 27—5 4 3 2 1

Contents

Prologue

Israel in Iran's Crosshairs

The Middle East stands at the precipice of a catastrophic conflict that could engulf the entire region. Nowhere is this threat more palpable than in the escalating tensions between Israel and Iran. These two nations are locked in an existential struggle with profound biblical and prophetic implications.

For years, Iran's relentless pursuit of nuclear weapons and unwavering hostility towards Israel have raised the specter of a massive military confrontation. The Iranian regime's inflammatory rhetoric, including calls for Israel's destruction by Supreme Leader Ayatollah Ali Khamenei and other top officials, has only heightened tensions in this high-stakes game of brinkmanship.

Over the years, Israel and Iran's longstanding rivalry has escalated into a shadow war, especially after Hamas's attack on Israel on October 7, 2023, followed by Israel's response in Gaza. Iranian-backed forces in Iraq and Syria have targeted US military positions for several months, with Iran's leadership linking these actions to Israel's Gaza operations. Concerns of a wider regional conflict surged in early April 2024, when Iran accused Israel of bombing its diplomatic complex in Syria on April 1, further fueling the volatile situation between the two adversaries.

On April 14, 2024, the simmering tensions between Israel and Iran erupted into open conflict, ushering in a dangerous new chapter for the adversaries. The unprecedented Iranian missile barrage against Israel on April 14 marked a chilling escalation in the long-simmering conflict between these two nations. For the first time, Iran directly attacked Israeli soil, launching over 170 drones, 30 cruise missiles, and 120 ballistic missiles from its own territory as well as from Iraq, Syria, and Yemen. This assault represented a stark departure from Iran's previous strategy of operating through proxies, signaling a perilous turning point in Middle Eastern geopolitics.

Israel's advanced air defenses, bolstered by assistance from the US, UK, France, and other allies, proved remarkably effective, intercepting an astounding 99 percent of the incoming projectiles. This demonstration of defensive capability, while reassuring, also highlighted the gravity of the threat Israel faces from its determined adversaries.

The Iranian regime's decision to launch such a brazen attack appeared to be motivated by a desire to project strength and deterrence capabilities. However, their actions only served to galvanize Israel's resolve. Just six days later, on April 19, the

Israeli military struck back with precision, targeting and severely damaging parts of Iran's Russian-made S-300 air defense system near the strategically important cities of Isfahan and Natanz.

These Israeli strikes were more than just a retaliatory measure; they sent a clear and potent message to Tehran. By successfully penetrating Iran's air defenses and threatening key nuclear sites like the uranium enrichment facility at Natanz, Israel demonstrated its capability to strike at the heart of Iran's most sensitive and heavily guarded assets. It amounted to a thinly veiled warning: curb your aggression or face devastating consequences to your nuclear program.

October 1, 2024, ushered in a new phase in the ongoing conflict between Iran and Israel. What began with air raid sirens sounding across central Israel quickly escalated into a situation that threatens to engulf the entire region in all-out war. As believers watching these events unfold, we must recognize their profound prophetic significance and prepare our hearts for what may come next.

Iran's second massive missile attack on Israel this year represents a brazen escalation of hostilities. Unlike the April assault, this latest barrage was an attempt to deliberately strike at the heart of Israel's urban centers, including the densely populated area around Tel Aviv. The attack came with little warning—just an hour before the sirens began to wail, US intelligence had warned Israel of an imminent missile attack expected within the next 12 hours.

The speed and scale of the assault were staggering. Iran launched a barrage of 181 ballistic missiles, which can reach their targets in Israel within a matter of minutes—some reports suggest as little as 11 to 12 minutes from launch to impact. This compressed timeframe left precious little room for defensive measures or evacuation efforts.

Despite the ferocity of the attack, Israel's advanced air defense systems, bolstered by US assistance, once again proved remarkably effective. They managed to intercept the vast majority of incoming missiles, limiting the damage on the ground. However, the psychological impact on the Israeli population cannot be overstated. The attack shattered any illusion of safety, even in the heart of Israel's most populous region.

In the immediate aftermath, Israel's response has been swift and decisive. The security cabinet convened an emergency meeting, and there's a growing consensus among military leaders, defense experts, and politicians that Israel must respond with unprecedented force. The restraint shown after the April attack is increasingly viewed as a miscalculation, one that Israel seems unwilling to repeat.

As of right now, Israel has not yet mustered a military response, but one is coming. By the time this book is published, Israel will have struck somewhere within Iran, although we don't know the specifics at the time of this writing.

As we reflect on these developments, we know the illusion of peace through measured responses has been shattered, and Israel now stands at a crossroads that could reshape the entire Middle East. The potential targets for Israel's retaliation are sobering to consider. There's talk of striking Iranian oil production facilities and military bases, actions that could have far-reaching economic and geopolitical consequences. While nuclear sites appear to be off the table for now, the scope of Israel's planned response suggests a willingness to risk a direct, prolonged, and costly conflict with Iran.

This escalation aligns astonishingly well with biblical prophecies concerning the End Times, particularly the Gog-Magog invasion foretold in Ezekiel chapters 38–39. We see Iran (ancient Persia) taking center stage in a coalition against Israel, just as Scripture foretold millennia ago. The involvement of other nations, including Russia's deepening alliance with Iran, further echoes the prophetic narrative.

The Israeli people, still grappling with the trauma of Hamas's attack one year ago on October 7, 2023, appear more willing than ever to accept short-term risks for the promise of long-term security. This shift in national psychology could have profound implications for the region and the world.

As tensions escalate and the prophetic clock ticks forward, believers must remain vigilant and prayerful. We stand in solidarity with Israel, praying for the peace of Jerusalem (Psalm 122:6). At the same time, we should not forget to pray for the Iranian people, many of whom do not share their government's hostility towards Israel.

As we watch these prophecies unfold, we choose to be filled with hope rather than fear. Even in the midst of increasing turmoil, we know that these are the birth pangs announcing the coming of our Lord. Though the nations rage and kingdoms falter, we are confident that

> The LORD of hosts is with us;
>   the God of Jacob is our fortress
>   (Psalm 46:7 ESV).

Introduction

Birth of a Rivalry

The bitter enmity between Israel and Iran is a new phenomenon in the greater sweep of history. While we will go into more detail later in this book, it's important to understand at the outset that the hostile relationship between the two nations is relatively recent. In ancient times, Israel and Persia (Iran's predecessor) actually had an often friendly, or at least neutral, relationship.

Cyrus the Great, one of ancient Persia's most illustrious rulers, was anointed by God to restore the Jewish people to their homeland after the Babylonian Captivity (2 Chronicles 36:22–23; Ezra 1:1–4; Isaiah 44:28; 45:1). He issued a remarkable decree that allowed the Jews to return to Israel and rebuild the Temple—a striking example of how God can use even a pagan king to fulfill His purposes.

Relations then remained largely cordial between the Jewish people and the ancient Persians and Medes for centuries. But things changed dramatically with the rise of anti-Semitism in early 20th century Iran, inflamed by Nazi propaganda. Anti-Jewish conspiracy theories and hate literature proliferated throughout the Iranian populace.

Still, under the reign of Shah Mohammed Reza Pahlavi from 1941 to 1979, Israel and Iran maintained generally positive ties. The secular-oriented Shah viewed Israel as a natural ally against the Arab nationalism championed by Egyptian President Gamal Abdel Nasser. Israel and Iran engaged in robust trade and military and intelligence cooperation.

All that changed with the 1979 Islamic Revolution, which brought to power a radical Shia theocracy. The Ayatollah Khomeini, Iran's first Supreme Leader after the 1979 revolution, declared Israel to be an illegitimate state that must be "wiped off the map." This remains the official position of the current Iranian regime under Supreme Leader Ayatollah Ali Khamenei.

The feud has steadily escalated over decades, with Iran and Israel trading covert blows while avoiding a direct confrontation until now. Iranian-backed Hezbollah rained rockets on Israel during the 2006 Lebanon War. In 2010, the Stuxnet computer virus—widely believed to be a joint US-Israeli cyberweapon—wreaked havoc on Iran's nuclear enrichment centrifuges. Mysterious explosions have struck sensitive Iranian nuclear and military sites. Iran and Israel have engaged in a maritime shadow war, targeting each other's commercial vessels.

Most significantly, Israel has conducted hundreds of airstrikes against Iranian forces and proxies in

Syria since intervening in the civil war in 2013 to prevent Iran from entrenching militarily on Israel's own doorstep. Iran retaliated by ordering its proxies like the Palestinian Islamic Jihad to fire rockets at Israel. Until this latest missile assault, Iran refrained from directly attacking Israel, relying instead on its proxies to do the fighting. Whenever hostilities flared, each side was careful to avoid crossing the other's red lines.

Now the old rules of the game appear to have been shattered. By launching missiles from its own soil, Iran has openly entered into direct confrontation with Israel, which had previously warned this would be a bridge too far. The risk of a miscalculation leading to a wider war has never been greater.

A Spiritual Conflict

The stakes could not be higher—and the dangers are not just geopolitical but also spiritual. Christians must recognize that at its core, the Israel-Iran conflict is not just a political or military rivalry but part of the cosmic struggle between good and evil. It is the ancient hatred held by Satan toward God's chosen people, a hatred that has repeatedly manifested throughout history from Pharaoh to Haman to Hitler.

In Iran's Islamist tyranny, we see this same murderous spirit dedicated to Israel's demise. The Iranian regime's Jew-hatred is deeply rooted in its extremist theology, which combines Shia Islam's end-times prophecies with a toxic stew of Nazi-inspired anti-Semitic conspiracy theories. It views itself as the righteous leader of the Muslim world in a holy war against the "Zionist entity." Israel's existence as the sole Jewish state is seen as an affront to Islam's supremacist ideology and a dagger plunged into the heart of the Muslim Middle East.

The Bible is clear that those who curse Israel bring judgment on themselves (Genesis 12:3). And the current Iranian regime has done far more than curse Israel. It has sought to annihilate the Jewish state through terror proxies, missiles, and the pursuit of nuclear weapons.

As such, Iran represents the latest incarnation of Satan's age-old yet eternally futile quest to destroy the Jewish people. God's enduring promise to Abraham remains as true as ever: "I will bless those who bless you, and him who dishonors you I will curse, and in you all the families of the earth shall be blessed" (Genesis 12:3). As Christians, we must bless and stand with Israel, especially in its hour of need, knowing that God will keep His covenant promise to preserve the Jewish people.

Throughout the Bible, God makes it clear that Israel will be restored as a nation in the last days, never again to be uprooted from its ancient homeland (Jeremiah 31:31–40; Ezekiel 36:22–28; Amos 9:14–15). The harrowing events of the Tribulation will devastate Israel, but a remnant will emerge to call on Yeshua as Messiah. All Israel will be saved (Zechariah 12:10; Romans 11:26).

So while the menacing shadow of Persia looms once more over Israel, we know it cannot thwart God's plan. The Bible contains piercing prophetic insight into Iran's end-times destiny, giving us hope even amid such perilous times.

Standing with Israel in the Face of Satanic Rage

Here is what we know: The Bible is clear that Israel will be supernaturally regathered in the last days from the four corners of the earth (Isaiah 11:12). This includes the lands of ancient Persia and Babylon, corresponding to modern-day Iran and Iraq. Israel will face a terrifying array of enemies determined to destroy her, chief among them Iran, part of a military confederacy that will attempt a massive invasion.

But the Lord will deliver Israel as He intervenes to defeat this coalition in spectacular fashion (Ezekiel 38–39). He will further vindicate Israel and its claims to the land by preserving a remnant to enter the Millennial Kingdom. This restored Israel will feature a reunited Judah and Ephraim, encompassing those returning from both the Assyrian and Babylonian exiles (Ezekiel 37; Obadiah 1:19–20).

Before Israel enters her promised destiny, she will first go through the crucible of the Tribulation. During this time, Iran's festering hatred of Israel will boil over, and the Jewish state will face the greatest threat to its existence, foreshadowed in the story of

Esther when wicked Haman devised a plot to annihilate the Jews throughout the Persian Empire.

Today, Haman's murderous spirit lives on in the halls of power in Tehran. Iran's Supreme Leader has called Israel a "cancerous tumor" that must be "removed and eradicated." An aide to the Iranian President has vowed that Iran's army will soon "liberate Haifa and Tel Aviv." Former Iranian President Mahmoud Ahmadinejad infamously said Israel must be "eliminated from the pages of history." The ominous chant of "Death to Israel!" resounds at every regime rally.

Yet Israel should take comfort knowing that just as in Esther's day, "relief and deliverance will rise for the Jews from another place" (Esther 4:14). The Persian gallows meant for the Jews ended up becoming the instrument of Haman's destruction. So too will the satanic plots of Iran's modern Hamans ultimately fail. Those who seek Israel's demise invite their own downfall and God's judgment.

In the meantime, followers of the Messiah have a sacred duty to bless and stand with Israel, especially as the specter of war looms. We must pray for the peace of Jerusalem (Psalm 122:6) and for the blindness to be removed from Jewish eyes (Romans 11:25) so they may recognize Yeshua as Messiah. And yes, we ought to pray for Iran's salvation too, for a great spiritual awakening that will transform this nation from a den of Israel-hatred to a wellspring of blessing.

Admittedly, in looking at the Middle East today, it's hard to see how that could happen. Iran's leadership remains relentlessly hostile to Israel, feverishly spinning centrifuges to potentially produce nuclear weapons, arming its terrorist proxies, and directly attacking Israel with drones and missiles in a dramatic escalation. Israel may well respond with punishing airstrikes on Iranian soil. Many fear the region is teetering on the brink of a catastrophic war.

Yet as Bible-believing Christians, we must view Israel and Iran through the lens of Scripture, not the 24/7 news cycle. In the dizzying swirl of headlines, let us never lose sight of God's prophetic plan. He is moving among the Jewish people and the nations to accomplish His purposes and hasten the Messiah's coming. And far from eternal enemies, the Bible holds out the hope of Israel and Iran (Persia) being gloriously reconciled under the lordship of the Prince of Peace.

Jeremiah foresaw a time when the descendants of Elam (ancient southwest Iran) will be regathered in the land (Jeremiah 49:39)—a poignant prophecy indeed as many Iranians suffer under oppression. Obadiah spoke of a restoration when Israelites will return and possess ancestral lands, including some from "Sepharad," possibly referring to Persia/southern Iran (Obadiah 1:20).

Instead of chanting, "Death to Israel" and Israelis responding, "Death to Iran," there is coming a day when a redeemed remnant from both peoples will together declare, "Blessed is He who comes in the name of Yahweh." May that day come soon.

As Christians committed to a biblical worldview, let us stand in solidarity with Israel while lifting up the Iranian people—a people so deeply loved by God that He is appearing to many of them in dreams and visions with the glorious gospel. The story of Iran and Israel is still being written, but we know the end: all nations will be blessed as the knowledge of the Lord covers the earth (Isaiah 11:9) and the ransomed stream to Zion (Isaiah 35:10).

Until that day, we choose faith over fear, anchored in God's unshakable promises. Iran's missile blitz is a wake-up call to be watchful and pray for Jerusalem's peace. It's a sobering reminder that the last days' birth pains are intensifying (Matthew 24:8). At this inflection point, let the Messiah's bride proclaim, "Israel, we stand with you! Iran, we're praying for you! Come Lord Yeshua! Maranatha!"

The Book's Overview

In the chapters that follow, we will explore the profound biblical and prophetic implications of the escalating crisis between Iran and Israel, shedding light on the ancient roots of this conflict and its potential role in the unfolding of end-times events.

Chapter 1 delves into the prophetic significance of the nations that will unite against Israel in the Gog-Magog invasion, as foretold by the prophet

Ezekiel, with a particular emphasis on the pivotal role of Iran (ancient Persia).

Chapter 2 takes us on a journey through the rich tapestry of Iran's interactions with the people of God throughout Scripture, from its formative role in the restoration of Jerusalem to the symbolic prophecies concerning its rise and fall.

In **Chapter 3,** we trace the turbulent history of Iran, from the glory days of the Persian Empire to the tumultuous events of the Islamic Revolution and the contemporary era, uncovering the cultural, religious, and political forces that have shaped Iran's contemporary worldview and positioned it as a leading adversary of Israel and the West.

Chapter 4 investigates the heart of biblical prophecy, unveiling Iran's central role in the prophesied Gog-Magog invasion of Israel, exploring the chilling details of Ezekiel's prophecy, and examining the alignment of current events with Bible prophecy.

Chapter 5 grapples with the complex question of timing, examining the various perspectives on when the Gog-Magog War might occur in relation to other end-times events, such as the Tribulation period and the rise of the Antichrist.

In **Chapter 6,** we confront the grave threat posed by a nuclear-armed Iran, exploring the apocalyptic ideologies that drive the regime's pursuit of atomic weapons and the existential danger this poses to Israel and the world.

Chapter 7 provides a vivid and chilling account of the Gog-Magog War itself, drawing upon the prophetic descriptions found in Ezekiel's writings, witnessing the unfolding of this cataclysmic event, God's divine intervention, and the profound aftermath that will reshape the geopolitical landscape.

Chapter 8 explores the details of how the stage is set for the Gog-Magog War and other end-times events, examining the convergence of geopolitical, cultural, and technological developments that align with biblical prophecy.

Finally, the **Conclusion** offers practical guidance on how Christians should live in these dangerous times, exhorting us to stand firm in our faith, remain steadfast in our witness, and embrace the urgency of the hour as we watch the unfolding of these momentous events.

As we traverse this treacherous terrain, may we be found faithful and prepared, proclaiming the hope of the gospel and standing firm in our faith until the day of Christ's appearing.

GOG-MAGOG COALITION

ANCIENT NAME	MODERN NAME	EZEKIEL
Rosh	Russia	38:2
Magog	Central Asia	38:2
Meshech	Turkey	38:2
Tubal	Turkey	38:2
Persia	Iran	38:5
Cush	Sudan & Ethiopia	38:5
Put	Libya	38:5
Gomer	Turkey	38:6
Togarmah	Turkey	38:6

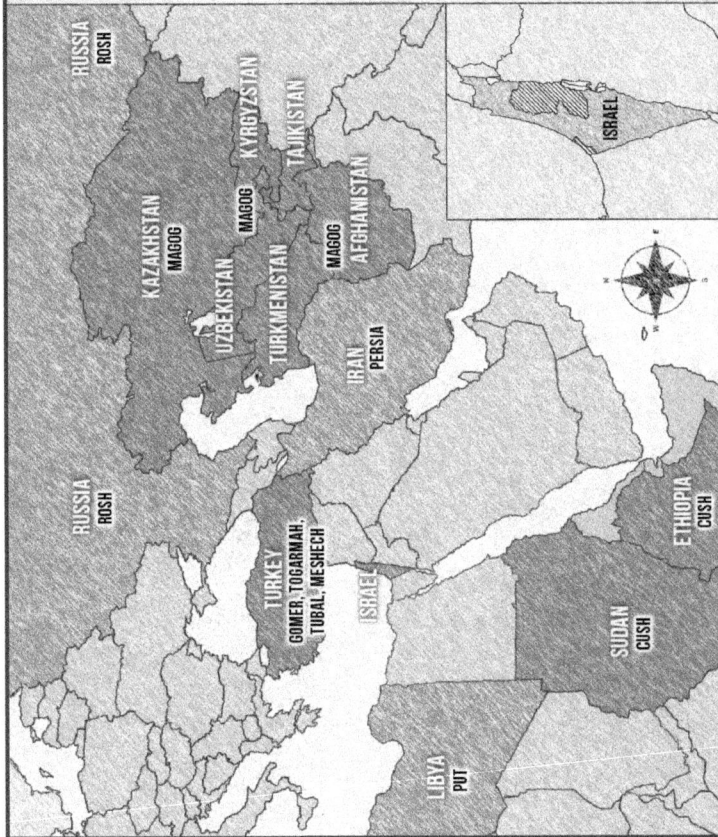

RUSSIA
ROSH

KYRGYZSTAN

TAJIKISTAN

KAZAKHSTAN
MAGOG

MAGOG

MAGOG
AFGHANISTAN

UZBEKISTAN

TURKMENISTAN

IRAN
PERSIA

ISRAEL

RUSSIA
ROSH

TURKEY
GOMER, TOGARMAH,
TUBAL, MESHECH

ISRAEL

ETHIOPIA
CUSH

SUDAN
CUSH

LIBYA
PUT

1

The Nations Aligned

The Prophecy of Ezekiel

Over 2,600 years ago, the ancient Hebrew prophet Ezekiel received a stunning revelation from God about a climactic event that would pit Israel against a formidable coalition of nations in the end-times. This prophetic invasion, often referred to as the "Gog-Magog War," is described in great detail in Ezekiel chapters 38 and 39. We recommend going to the back of this book to read the Scripture index for the complete text of these chapters. The prophecy begins with a stern warning from the Lord to Ezekiel:

> Now the word of the LORD came to me, saying, "Son of man, set your face against Gog, of the land of Magog, the prince of Rosh, Meshech, and Tubal, and prophesy against him, and say, 'Thus says the Lord GOD: "Behold, I *am* against you, O Gog, the prince of Rosh, Meshech, and Tubal. I will turn you around, put hooks into your jaws, and lead you out, with all your army, horses, and horsemen, all splendidly clothed, a

great company *with* bucklers and shields, all of them handling swords. Persia, Ethiopia, and Libya are with them, all of them *with* shield and helmet; Gomer and all its troops; the house of Togarmah *from* the far north and all its troops—many people *are* with you" (Ezekiel 38:1–6 NKJV).

The prophecy goes on to list the specific nations that will join this coalition against Israel, including Rosh (Russia), Magog (central Asia), Persia (modern-day Iran), Meshach and Tubal (Turkey), Cush (Sudan and Ethiopia), Put (Libya), and Gomer and Beth-togarmah (regions of modern-day Turkey). Ezekiel concludes his list by saying there will be "many peoples" who also join the coalition. Some translations say they are "many nations." These other peoples in verse 6 could be other nations or mercenary proxies, such as Hamas, Hezbollah, Houthis, and any other group that might join the Muslim "Axis of Resistance" against Israel.

There is one specific issue we must address with Ezekiel's list of nations. The translation of the Hebrew word *rosh* in Ezekiel 38 has been a point of debate among Bible scholars. In this passage, Ezekiel used this word in reference to "Gog, the prince of Rosh, Meshech, and Tubal" (vv. 2–3 NKJV). The King James Version translated *rosh* as an adjective meaning 'chief,' rendering it "the chief prince of Meshech and Tubal."

However, some modern translations treat *Rosh* as a proper noun, referring to a geographical location or people group. The NKJV and others follow the interpretation that *Rosh* may be an ancient name for an area in what is now Russia or regions around the Black Sea.

This understanding aligns with other ancient texts and inscriptions that seem to use *Rosh* in a geographical sense. While not conclusive, many scholars find this a plausible translation given the context of the surrounding nations mentioned. The specific identity of *Rosh* remains uncertain, but the notion of it being a proper noun for a place or people has gained wider acceptance in recent centuries. Our position is that Rosh is a reference to the geographical area roughly known as Russia.

While the names used in Ezekiel's prophecy are ancient, modern scholarship and geopolitical developments have shed light on their identities in today's world. This biblical forewarning, written over two and a half millennia ago, takes on profound significance when we consider the remarkable alignment of nations in our modern world.

The Key Players

According to Ezekiel 38:1–6, the primary nations that will align themselves against Israel in this future invasion include:

Nations of the Gog-Magog War		
Ancient Name	Modern Name	Biblical Reference
Rosh	Russia	Ezekiel 38:2
Magog	Central Asia	Ezekiel 38:2
Meshech	Turkey	Ezekiel 38:2
Tubal	Turkey	Ezekiel 38:2
Persia	Iran	Ezekiel 38:5
Cush	Sudan & Ethiopia	Ezekiel 38:5
Put	Libya	Ezekiel 38:5
Gomer	Turkey	Ezekiel 38:6
Togarmah	Turkey	Ezekiel 38:6

Remarkably, as we examine the current geopolitical landscape, we see a striking alignment of these very nations, with deep ties to Russia and a shared hostility towards Israel.

Russia and Iran: A Strategic Partnership

Iran, a central player in this prophetic conflict, has been unwavering in its pursuit of nuclear weapons and its stated goal of wiping Israel off the map. Its support for terrorist groups like Hezbollah, Hamas, and the Houthis and its growing influence in the region have made it a formidable threat to Israel's security.

Russia, on the other hand, has forged strong alliances with Iran and Syria, providing military support and shielding these nations from international pressure. The ties between Iran and Russia are growing closer every day, united by their shared animosity toward Israel and the West.

This partnership between Russia and Iran is not merely a matter of geopolitical convenience; it has deep historical and ideological roots too. Iran's Islamic Republic has long sought to position itself as a leading voice in the Muslim world, challenging Western influence and promoting an anti-Israel agenda. Russia, too, has sought to reassert its global influence and challenge the Western-led world order.

Moreover, both nations have a vested interest in maintaining a foothold in the Middle East, with Russia seeking to protect its strategic interests in Syria and Iran seeking to expand its influence throughout the region. This alignment of interests has led to a deepening of military and economic cooperation between the two nations, further solidifying their partnership.

Turkey's Shifting Allegiances

Turkey, a NATO member, has also been moving closer to Russia and Iran, increasingly at odds with its traditional Western allies. While Turkey currently maintains a friendly relationship with Israel, this could change if it is spurned by the European Union or other Western powers.

Turkey's President Recep Tayyip Erdogan has pursued an increasingly assertive and independent foreign policy, seeking to position Turkey as a regional power and a leader in the Muslim world. This has led to tensions with the United States and other NATO allies, who have expressed concerns about Turkey's growing ties with Russia and Iran.

Furthermore, Turkey has been engaged in a long-standing conflict with Kurdish separatist groups, some of which are supported by the United States and its allies. This has strained relations between Turkey and the West even more, pushing Turkey closer to Russia and Iran, who share Turkey's concerns about Kurdish independence movements.

The Role of Sudan and Libya

The involvement of Sudan and Libya in this prophetic conflict may seem puzzling, but both nations have been deeply influenced by radical Islamic ideologies and have a history of supporting terrorist organizations. Sudan and Libya are also strategically positioned in North Africa, providing potential staging grounds for an invasion of Israel from the south.

Sudan, in particular, has been a hotbed of Islamic extremism and has served as a haven for groups like Al-Qaeda and other terrorist organizations. The country's longstanding conflict with its Christian and non-Arab populations has further fueled extremist ideologies and anti-Western sentiments.

Libya, too, has been plagued by instability and the rise of radical Islamic groups in the aftermath of the Arab Spring and the fall of Muammar Gaddafi's regime. The country's porous borders and vast ungoverned spaces have made it a fertile breeding ground for terrorist organizations and a potential staging area for attacks against Israel and its allies.

Both Sudan and Libya have also been drawn into the orbit of Russia and Iran, seeking military and economic support from these powers in the face of international isolation and sanctions. This alignment of interests serves to solidify their potential role in the prophesied Gog-Magog coalition.

The Prophetic Significance

Ezekiel's prophecies take on profound significance when we consider the remarkable alignment of nations in our modern world. The fact that these specific nations, separated by vast distances and diverse cultures, are now converging in their hostility towards Israel is a striking fulfillment of biblical predictions made over two and a half millennia ago.

Even more, Ezekiel emphasized that the invasion force would come from the "far north" (Ezekiel 38:6, 15; 39:2). If you draw a straight line north of Jerusalem, you'll hit Moscow. No other nation is as geographically north of Israel as Russia. This detail, seemingly insignificant in Ezekiel's time, now carries immense prophetic weight.

The prophet's detailed descriptions of the military might and advanced weaponry of the invading forces also resonate with the modern capabilities of nations like Russia and Iran. Ezekiel speaks of "horses and horsemen," "bucklers and shields," and "swords" (Ezekiel 38:4), which may be references to the advanced military hardware and technology of our time.

God's Sovereign Plan

One of the most striking aspects of Ezekiel's prophecy is the assertion that God Himself will orchestrate and direct this invasion of Israel. The Lord declares, "And I will turn you about and put hooks into your jaws, and I will bring you out, and all your army, horses and horsemen, all of them clothed in full armor, a great host, all of them with buckler and shield, wielding swords" (Ezekiel 38:4). The "hooks into the jaws" metaphor speaks of God's sovereign control over the nations, compelling them to act according to His divine plan.

While the nations involved in this alliance may believe they are acting of their own volition, driven by their hatred for Israel or their pursuit of power and resources, the Bible makes it clear that God is the One who will ultimately provoke and drive them to fulfill His prophetic purposes.

This aspect of the prophecy serves as a powerful reminder that God is in control of human history, and even the most powerful nations and leaders are mere instruments in His hand. It also underscores the fact that the events unfolding in our world today are not merely the result of human machinations but rather part of a larger, divinely ordained plan.

Some scholars have suggested that the "hooks in the jaws" metaphor may refer to specific events or circumstances that will serve as catalysts for the Gog-Magog invasion. For example, the recent assassination of Iranian General Qasem Soleimani by the United States or the ongoing tensions between Iran and Israel over Iran's nuclear program could be seen as potential "hooks" that may draw these nations into conflict.

The Geopolitical Landscape

To fully appreciate the prophetic significance of the Gog-Magog invasion, it is important to understand the geopolitical landscape in which these events are unfolding. The modern-day Middle East is a complex tapestry of competing interests, shifting alliances, and deep-seated ideological and religious tensions.

The Rise of Islamic Extremism
One of the defining features of the contemporary Middle East is the rise of Islamic extremism, fueled by groups like Al-Qaeda, ISIS, and others. These organizations have exploited the instability and power vacuums that have emerged in the region, often capitalizing on the grievances of marginalized populations and the failure of secular governments to address economic and social challenges.

The proliferation of extremist ideologies has not only destabilized the region but has also created a fertile breeding ground for anti-Israel sentiment and rhetoric. Groups like Hamas and Hezbollah, which are backed by Iran, have made the destruction of Israel a central tenet of their ideological platforms, further fueling the potential for conflict.

The Struggle for Regional Dominance

Another key factor shaping the geopolitical landscape is the ongoing struggle for regional dominance among the major powers in the Middle East. Iran, in particular, has sought to position itself as the preeminent force in the region, leveraging its support for proxy groups and its pursuit of nuclear weapons to bolster its influence.

Saudi Arabia and other Gulf states, on the other hand, have sought to counter Iran's ambitions, often aligning themselves with the United States and other Western powers. This competition for regional domination has further exacerbated tensions and increased the risk of conflict.

The Role of Russia and China

In addition to the internal dynamics of the Middle East, the region has also become a battleground for the competing interests of global powers like Russia and China. Both nations have sought to establish footholds in the region, often through the provision of military aid and economic support to countries like Syria and Iran.

Russia, in particular, has played a pivotal role in the Syrian conflict, intervening militarily to prop up the regime of Bashar al-Assad and maintain its strategic interests in the region. This has brought Russia into direct confrontation with the United States and its allies, further complicating the geo-political landscape.

China, too, has sought to expand its influence in the Middle East, driven by its insatiable demand for energy resources and its desire to assert itself as a global superpower. The Belt and Road Initiative, China's ambitious infrastructure and development program, has provided a vehicle for deepening economic ties with nations throughout the region.

The Curtain Opening

With the miraculous rebirth of Israel in 1948 and the more recent aligning of the Gog-Magog nations, the stage is now set and the curtain is opening for this long-foretold conflict. Many prophecy experts believe it is one of the next major prophetic events on the horizon. While we cannot set dates, the prophetic dominoes are falling into place at an unprecedented pace.

The recent attack by Iran, a key member of the Gog-Magog axis, against Israel in April 2024 feels like the prelude to the main act. As the world watches the simmering conflict between Iran and Israel with bated breath, wondering if it will boil over into full-scale war, we believe it is time for believers everywhere to wake up and prepare, not just physically but spiritually too. The ultimate fulfillment of Ezekiel 38–39 may be closer than many realize.

The Road Ahead

As we have seen in this chapter, the nations prophesied by Ezekiel to align against Israel in the end-times are indeed coming together, just as the Bible foretold over 2,600 years ago. This remarkable foreshadowing of ancient prophecy serves as a stark reminder that the events unfolding in our world today are part of a larger, divinely orchestrated plan.

The convergence of these nations, each with its own complex history and geopolitical ambitions, is a testament to the accuracy and relevance of God's Word. It also underscores the fact that the conflicts and tensions we see in the Middle East today are not mere happenstance but rather part of a prophetic tapestry woven over millennia.

In the next chapter, we will dig deeper into the role of Iran in this prophetic scenario, exploring its historical and scriptural significance, as well as the potential timing and aftermath of the Gog-Magog War. We will examine the ideological and theological underpinnings of Iran's hostility towards Israel, and how this animosity has been shaped by the nation's unique blend of Islamic theology and Persian culture.

We will also explore the potential consequences of a military conflict between Iran and Israel, and how such a conflict could escalate into a broader regional or even global conflagration. Additionally, we will consider the potential for divine intervention, as foretold in Ezekiel's prophecy, and how God's sovereign hand may ultimately bring about the resolution of this age-old conflict.

As we weather these tumultuous times, it is essential for us to keep our eyes fixed on the unchanging truth of God's Word and the promise of His ultimate redemptive plan for Israel and the nations. The events unfolding in the Middle East, while often unsettling and complex, are part of a grand narrative that has been unfolding since the dawn of human history. It is our privilege and responsibility as believers to bear witness to these events and to proclaim the hope and assurance that can only be found in the God of Abraham, Isaac, and Jacob.

2

Iran in Scripture

After exploring the nations aligned against Israel in the prophesied Gog-Magog invasion, we now turn our full attention to the pivotal role of Iran (ancient Persia) in biblical history and prophecy. While the name "Iran" does not appear in Scripture, the land and people of Persia are mentioned numerous times, especially throughout the Old Testament. Understanding Iran's profound significance as portrayed in the Bible is crucial for grasping the unfolding of end-times events and recognizing the prophetic signs of the times we are living in.

Persia's Formative Interactions with Israel

The first references to Persia in Scripture highlight the prominent military might of the Persian people, even in ancient times. In Ezekiel 27:10, the prophet speaks of soldiers from Persia serving as mercenary forces in the Phoenician city of Tyre, renowned for its fortifications and maritime power. This early mention sets the stage for Persia's subsequent interactions with God's chosen nation, Israel, and its integral role in the outworking of biblical prophecy.

One of the most consequential interactions between Persia and the people of Israel is recorded in the books of Ezra and Nehemiah. Here, we encounter the Persian king Cyrus the Great, whose reign marked a pivotal turning point in Israel's history. In the first chapter of Ezra, we read the remarkable account of Cyrus's decree that allowed the Jewish exiles to return to Jerusalem from their Babylonian Captivity and rebuild their holy Temple, which had been destroyed decades earlier by the Babylonian armies (Ezra 1:1–4).

This act of benevolence and favor toward the Jewish people was not merely a political gesture but a fulfillment of an astonishing prophecy uttered by Isaiah over a century earlier. In Isaiah 44:28 and 45:1, the prophet refers to Cyrus as God's "shepherd" and "anointed one," foretelling his role in facilitating the return of the Jewish exiles to their homeland. This remarkable prophecy, accurately predicting the rise of Cyrus and his subsequent actions, stands as a powerful testament to the divine inspiration of Scripture and God's sovereignty over the affairs of nations.

Throughout the books of Ezra and Nehemiah, we witness the ongoing and complex interactions between the successive Persian kings and the Jewish people as they worked to rebuild Jerusalem and reestablish their religious and cultural heritage. While some kings, like Darius and Artaxerxes, supported and enabled the rebuilding efforts, others, such as Ahasuerus (known as Xerxes in secular history), were influenced by the enemies of the Jews and sought to hinder their progress through oppressive decrees and policies (Ezra 4, Esther 3).

The book of Esther provides a remarkable account of God's providential protection over His people living in the Persian Empire during the reign of Ahasuerus. The narrative revolves around the diabolical plot of Haman, a high-ranking Persian official, to annihilate the Jewish population throughout the empire. Through the courage and faith of Esther, a Jewish woman who became the queen of Persia, and her cousin Mordecai, God intervened in a miraculous way to preserve His people and bring about the downfall of their enemies. This deliverance is commemorated annually by the Jewish Feast of Purim, a lasting reminder of God's faithfulness and sovereignty over the affairs of nations and individuals.

These formative interactions between Persia and the people of Israel, recorded in the historical books of the Old Testament, lay the groundwork for understanding the profound prophetic significance of this ancient empire in the unfolding of God's redemptive plan for humanity.

Prophecies of Persia's Rise and Fall

While the historical accounts of the Old Testament reveal Persia's pivotal role in the lives of God's people, the prophetic books, particularly the writings of Daniel and Ezekiel, contain rich symbolic representations and specific prophecies concerning the rise, dominion, and eventual downfall of the Persian Empire.

In the book of Daniel, we encounter multiple visions and prophecies that foretell the ascendancy of the Persian Empire and its place in the succession of world powers. In Daniel 2, the prophet interprets Nebuchadnezzar's famous dream of a great statue, where the chest and arms of silver represent the Persian Empire that would succeed and conquer the Babylonian Empire, symbolized by the head of gold (Daniel 2:32, 39).

Later, in Daniel 7, the prophet receives a vision of four beasts arising from the sea, each representing a world empire. The second beast, a lopsided bear with three ribs in its mouth, is explicitly identified as the Persian Empire (Daniel 7:5, 17). The symbolism of the bear's lopsided posture and the three ribs in its mouth is widely understood to represent the dual nature of the Medo-Persian Empire, comprised of the Median and Persian kingdoms, and the three most significant nations it conquered: Lydia (situated in modern-day Turkey), Babylon (Iraq), and Egypt.

Daniel 8 provides an even more detailed prophetic vision concerning the rise and fall of the Persian Empire. In this chapter, the prophet sees a vision of a two-horned ram, with one horn higher than the other, representing the Median and Persian components of the empire (Daniel 8:3, 20). The vision depicts the ram charging westward, northward, and southward, symbolizing the Persian Empire's expansionist conquests in all directions, until it is suddenly and violently destroyed by a male goat, representing the swift and decisive conquest of Persia by the Greek Empire under Alexander the Great (Daniel 8:5-8, 21–22).

The astonishing accuracy with which these prophecies were actually fulfilled in the rise, dominance, and eventual downfall of the Persian Empire at the hands of the Greeks provides a compelling testament to the divine inspiration of Scripture and the reliability of its prophetic utterances. These prophecies not only validate the historical narratives concerning Persia's interactions with Israel but also establish a precedent for the literal fulfillment of the remaining prophecies concerning Persia's (Iran's) future role in the unfolding of end-times events.

Iran's Central Role in Gog-Magog

One of the most significant and widely discussed prophecies concerning Persia's (Iran's) future involvement in the events leading up to the return of Christ is found in the prophetic passages of Ezekiel chapters 38–39, often referred to as the "Gog-Magog War" or the "War of Gog and Magog." In these chapters, the prophet Ezekiel foretells a massive, multinational invasion of Israel by a coalition of nations led by a powerful figure referred to as "Gog, of the land of Magog, the prince of Rosh, Meshech, and Tubal" (Ezekiel 38:2 NKJV).

Among the nations explicitly listed as part of this formidable alliance is Persia, or modern-day Iran (Ezekiel 38:5). While the identities of some of the other ancient places, such as Rosh, Meshech, and Tubal, are debated among scholars, there is a strong consensus that they likely represent regions and territories associated with modern-day Russia and the former Soviet republics. Other nations mentioned in the prophecy, such as Cush (understood to be ancient Ethiopia/Sudan), Put (ancient Libya), and Gomer and Beth-togarmah (associated with modern-day Turkey), further reinforce the prophetic significance of this multinational coalition.

Remarkably, the prominent members of this prophesied alliance—Russia, Iran, and Turkey—have become increasingly close strategic partners in recent years, particularly through their joint military cooperation in the Syrian conflict. This geopolitical realignment has brought these nations into close proximity with Israel's northern border, setting the stage for the potential fulfillment of Ezekiel's prophecy concerning the Gog-Magog invasion.

The Bible provides additional insights into the motivations and objectives of this coalition, led by the enigmatic figure Gog. Ezekiel 38:10–13 suggests that the invading forces will be driven by a desire for plunder and conquest, seeking to seize the wealth and resources of a prosperous and secure Israel. This chilling portrayal aligns with the well-documented ambitions of the current Iranian regime to expand its influence and control over the region, as well as its longstanding hostility toward the nation of Israel.

The prophecy also highlights the supernatural nature of God's intervention in defense of His people, promising to "summon a sword against Gog on all my mountains" (Ezekiel 38:21) and "with pestilence and bloodshed I will enter into judgment with him, and I will rain upon him and his hordes and the many peoples who are with him torrential rains and hailstones, fire and sulfur" (Ezekiel 38:22). This divine intervention will ultimately lead to the utter defeat and destruction of the invading forces, leaving them as "plunder" for Israel (Ezekiel 39:10) and serving as a powerful testimony to the nations of God's sovereignty and unwavering commitment to the preservation of His chosen people (Ezekiel 39:21–22).

While the precise timing of this prophesied invasion remains a matter of ongoing debate and speculation, which we will discuss later in the book, the Gog-Magog prophecy stands as a solemn reminder of Iran's central role in the unfolding of end-times events and the imminent fulfillment of God's redemptive plan for Israel and the world.

New Testament References

The New Testament, while primarily focused on the life, ministry, and teachings of Jesus Christ and the establishment of the early church, also contains subtle references and implications that may shed light on the ongoing significance of Persia (Iran) in the unfolding of God's redemptive plan.

One such reference is found in Acts 2:9, where Luke mentions that Parthian Jews were present in Jerusalem on the Day of Pentecost, witnessing the outpouring of the Holy Spirit and the birth of the Church. The Parthian Empire, which ruled over the territory of modern-day Iran from the third century BC to the third century AD, was a dominant power in the ancient world and played a significant role in the geopolitical landscape of the region during the time of Christ and the early Church.

While this reference may seem incidental, it serves as a reminder that the Persian people, and by extension the territory of modern-day Iran, were part of the broader Jewish diaspora and would continue to be interwoven into the unfolding of God's redemptive plan for humanity. From Pentecost onward, a gospel witness has remained in Iran.

Additionally, the book of Revelation, which unveils the prophetic events leading up to the return of Christ and the establishment of His eternal Kingdom, contains symbolic references that some scholars interpret as potential allusions to the involvement of Persia (Iran) in the end-times.

For instance, the mention of "the kings from the east" in Revelation 16:12, who are described as having their way prepared by the drying up of the Euphrates River, has been interpreted by some as a reference to nations in the Middle East, potentially including Iran. While the specific identities of these "kings of the east" are not explicitly stated, their inclusion in the prophetic narrative suggests their involvement in the events surrounding the final Battle of Armageddon and the return of Christ.

Furthermore, the repeated emphasis on the global nature of the end-times events and the gathering of "all the nations" against Jerusalem (Zechariah 14:2, Revelation 16:14) implies the potential involvement of Iran, a powerful and influential nation in the Middle East region, in the prophesied conflicts and upheavals that will precede the establishment of Christ's eternal Kingdom.

As we pore over these scriptural references and symbolic allusions, it becomes increasingly evident that Persia (Iran) has played a pivotal role in biblical history and will continue to occupy a central place in the unfolding of end-times events, particularly as they relate to the nation of Israel and the fulfillment of God's redemptive plan for humanity.

In the next chapter, we will go deeper into the rich and complex history of Persia (Iran), tracing its origins from the ancient Achaemenid Empire to the modern Islamic Republic. By examining Iran's cultural, religious, and political foundations, we will gain a better understanding of the factors that have shaped its current worldview, its turbulent relationship with Israel, and its geopolitical ambitions in the Middle East region.

This historical exploration will provide invaluable context for interpreting the prophetic significance of Iran's role in the unfolding of end-times events, as outlined in the preceding scriptural references. By bridging the gap between biblical prophecy and the historical realities of the modern Iranian regime, we will be better equipped to discern the signs of the times and prepare ourselves for the momentous events that lie ahead.

3

Iran in History

In the previous chapter, we looked at the profound significance of Persia (modern-day Iran) in biblical history and prophecy. From the remarkable fulfillment of Isaiah's prophecy concerning Cyrus the Great's decree allowing the Jewish exiles to return to Jerusalem, to the detailed visions and symbolic representations foretelling the rise and fall of the Persian Empire, Iran's ancient roots are deeply interwoven with the unfolding of God's redemptive plan.

However, to fully comprehend Iran's central role in the events leading up to the return of Christ and the establishment of His eternal Kingdom, it is essential to understand the rich tapestry of this nation's tumultuous history. By exploring the cultural, religious, and political forces that have shaped the Iranian psyche over millennia, we can gain invaluable insights into the contemporary worldview and geopolitical ambitions that make Iran a pivotal player in the prophetic drama yet to unfold.

The Achaemenid Dynasty

The origins of the Persian Empire can be traced back to the sixth century BC, when Cyrus the Great, the founder of the Achaemenid Dynasty, united the ancient kingdoms of the Medes and Persians and established one of the largest and most influential empires of antiquity. This vast realm, stretching from the Mediterranean Sea to the Indus River, encompassed a diverse array of cultures, peoples, and belief systems.

Under the reigns of Cyrus and his successors, such as Darius the Great and Xerxes I, the Persian Empire reached its zenith, known for its impressive infrastructure, architectural marvels like the magnificent city of Persepolis, and its advancements in governance, law, and administration. The empire's reach and influence extended far beyond its geographical boundaries, leaving an indelible mark on the course of human history.

The Persian Empire's interactions with the Jewish people were complex and often tumultuous, reflecting the intricate tapestry of religious and cultural forces that shaped the ancient world. While Cyrus allowed the exiled Jews to return to Jerusalem and rebuild their Temple, as foretold by the prophet Isaiah (Isaiah 45:1), subsequent rulers, such as Ahasuerus (Xerxes I), were influenced by enemies of the Jews and sought to hinder their progress through oppressive decrees and policies, as recounted in the book of Esther.

The Hellenistic Era

The Persian Empire's reign came to an end in 330 BC when the conquering forces of Alexander the Great swept through the region, fulfilling the prophecy in Daniel 8 concerning the swift and decisive conquest of Persia by the Greek Empire. This marked the beginning of the Hellenistic era, characterized by the spread of Greek culture, philosophy, and governance throughout the ancient world.

The impact of Greek civilization on the Iranian plateau was profound, with the region becoming a battleground for the competing interests of the Seleucid and Parthian dynasties. This period witnessed a rich exchange of ideas, art, and cultural influences, further shaping the Iranian identity and laying the foundations for future developments.

The Arrival of Islam

In the seventh century AD, a new force emerged that would forever alter the course of Iranian history—the advent of Islam. The Arab conquests swept across the region, ushering in a new era of religious and cultural transformation. The ancient Persian Empire gradually gave way to a series of Islamic dynasties, including the Abbasids, Seljuks, and Safavids, each leaving its unique imprint on the Iranian landscape.

The spread of Islam brought with it not only a new religion but also a new system of governance, laws, and societal norms. The Persian people, with their rich pre-Islamic heritage, adapted and integrated Islamic principles into their cultural fabric, creating a unique synthesis that would shape the nation's identity for centuries to come.

Throughout this period, the Iranian people maintained a strong sense of cultural identity and pride, even as they embraced the tenets of the Islamic faith. This delicate balance between preserving ancient traditions and adopting new religious and cultural influences would become a defining characteristic of the Iranian psyche, one that would have profound implications for the nation's future trajectory.

The Qajar Dynasty

The 19th century witnessed the rise of the Qajar dynasty, a period marked by increasing interactions with the West and the gradual modernization of Iranian society. This era saw the nation grapple with the challenges of maintaining its cultural and religious identity while navigating the currents of global change and technological advancements.

The Qajar rulers sought to reform and strengthen the Iranian state, introducing new administrative structures, educational systems, and military institutions. However, their efforts were often hampered by internal power struggles, economic challenges, and the growing influence of European powers in the region.

The Pahlavi Dynasty

The 20th century ushered in a new era for Iran with the establishment of the Pahlavi dynasty in 1925. Under Reza Shah Pahlavi, the nation underwent a period of rapid modernization and secularization, with efforts to centralize power, promote industrialization, and align Iran more closely with the West.

Reza Shah's reign was marked by a concerted effort to distance Iran from its Islamic heritage and promote a sense of national identity rooted in the country's pre-Islamic Persian past. This included the renaming of Persia to Iran, a deliberate attempt to associate the nation with the Aryan race and forge closer ties with Nazi Germany in the 1930s.

The Pahlavi era witnessed significant economic and social reforms, including the emancipation of women and the expansion of educational opportunities. However, these changes were often imposed in a heavy-handed manner, alienating segments of the population, and fueling resentment towards the monarchy and its perceived subservience to Western powers.

The 1979 Islamic Revolution

The late 1970s saw a confluence of factors that would ultimately lead to the overthrow of the Pahlavi dynasty and the establishment of the Islamic Republic of Iran. Rising economic challenges, coupled with growing dissatisfaction with the Shah's autocratic rule and the perceived erosion of Iranian cultural and religious values, created a powder keg of discontent.

It was against this backdrop that Ayatollah Ruhollah Khomeini emerged as the charismatic leader of the Islamic Revolution, galvanizing a diverse coalition of Iranians with his message of restoring Iran's Islamic identity and throwing off the shackles of Western influence.

The 1979 Islamic Revolution marked a seismic shift in Iran's political and religious landscape, ushering in a new era of hostility towards Israel, the United States, and the West. Khomeini swiftly severed ties with Israel, condemned Zionism as an "enemy of Islam," and transferred the Israeli embassy in Tehran to the Palestine Liberation Organization (PLO).

This dramatic reversal of Iran's relationship with Israel, which had previously enjoyed strong economic and military ties under the Shah's regime, set the stage for the nation's emergence as a leading voice in the anti-Israel movement and a staunch supporter of terrorist organizations like Hezbollah and Hamas.

Hegemony and Hostility

Since the 1979 revolution, Iran has pursued an increasingly aggressive and destabilizing foreign policy, fueled by its ambitions for regional hegemony and its unwavering hostility towards Israel and the West. The regime has actively cultivated ties with militant Islamic groups across the globe, earning it the dubious distinction of being the world's foremost state sponsor of terrorism.

Iran's involvement in regional conflicts and its support for proxy groups like Hezbollah and Hamas have further destabilized the Middle East, raising concerns among neighboring countries and the international community. The regime's efforts to undermine stability in Iraq, Afghanistan, Syria, and Yemen, as well as its growing influence in the region, have positioned it as a major threat to regional security and stability.

At the heart of Iran's belligerence lies its long-standing pursuit of nuclear weapons and its stated goal of wiping Israel off the map. Despite crushing economic sanctions and covert operations by Israel and others to hinder its nuclear program, Iran has relentlessly marched towards acquiring atomic weapons, viewing them as a means of securing its regional dominance and neutralizing the perceived threat posed by Israel and the West.

The 2015 nuclear deal, intended to curtail Iran's nuclear ambitions, was soon mired in controversy, with Iran accused of violating the terms of the agreement and continuing its pursuit of nuclear capabilities under the guise of compliance. The regime's inflammatory rhetoric, including calls for the destruction of Israel by Supreme Leader Ayatollah Ali Khamenei and other top officials, has only heightened tensions and raised the specter of a catastrophic confrontation.

As we examine the tapestry of Iran's rich and turbulent history, a clear pattern emerges: a nation grappling with the complexities of its ancient heritage,
its religious identity, and its quest for regional dominance. From the glory days of the Persian Empire
to the tumultuous events of the Islamic Revolution
and the contemporary era, Iran has been a crucible of
clashing civilizations, ideologies, and power struggles.

It is against this backdrop that the nation's role
in the unfolding of end-times prophecy takes on
profound significance. The historical forces that
have shaped Iran's contemporary worldview and
positioned it as a leading adversary of Israel and the
West are not mere happenstance but rather part of
a divine tapestry woven over millennia.

As we examine the complexities of the current
geopolitical landscape and the mounting tensions
between Iran and Israel, it is essential to view these
developments through the lens of biblical prophecy
and the eternal purposes of God. The stage is being
set for the fulfillment of Ezekiel's chilling vision of
the Gog-Magog invasion, with Iran poised to play a
central role in this prophetic drama.

In the next chapter, we will explore the specific
prophecies concerning Iran's (Persia's) involvement
in the Gog-Magog conflict, examine the scriptural
evidence, and interpret the signs of our times in
light of God's eternal Word. As we do so, may we
be reminded of the sovereign hand of God at work,
orchestrating the affairs of nations to bring about
His redemptive plan for Israel and the world.

4

Iran in Prophecy

In the previous chapter, we explored the rich and turbulent history of Iran, tracing its origins from the ancient Achaemenid Empire to the modern Islamic Republic. We probed the cultural, religious, and political forces that have shaped the Iranian psyche over millennia, providing invaluable context for understanding the nation's contemporary worldview, its tumultuous relationship with Israel, and its geopolitical ambitions in the Middle East region.

As we turn our attention to the prophetic significance of Iran, we must acknowledge that the nation's future is inextricably linked to the unfolding of end-times events foretold in Bible prophecy. Iran, known as Persia in biblical times, occupies a unique and pivotal position in prophecy, with numerous references and allusions scattered throughout the Old and New Testaments.

The Ezekiel Prophecy

One of the most compelling prophecies concerning Iran's future is found in the book of Ezekiel, chapters 38 and 39. In this passage, the prophet Ezekiel foretells a massive invasion of Israel by a coalition of nations led by the mysterious figure "Gog, of the land of Magog" (Ezekiel 38:2). Among the nations explicitly listed as part of this coalition is "Persia," the ancient name for the region now known as Iran (Ezekiel 38:5).

The implications of this prophecy are profound. Iran will play a central role in a future conflict that will pit a coalition of nations against the State of Israel. This prophecy has taken on increased significance in recent years through Iran's pursuit of nuclear weapons and its unwavering hostility towards Israel. Now that Iran has attacked Israel on its own soil, all these factors seem to be on a collision course with divine destiny.

The Prophetic Alignment

Ezekiel's prophecy provides a remarkable glimpse into the geopolitical landscape of the last days, with several key details aligning with the current realities in the Middle East:

1. Iran's Hostility Toward Israel

Since the 1979 Islamic Revolution, Iran's leaders have repeatedly called for Israel's destruction. They refer to Israel as the "Little Satan" and a "cancerous tumor" that needs to be eradicated. This seething hatred will culminate in Iran's enthusiastic participation in the prophesied invasion of Israel.

2. Military Preparations

Iran has been actively preparing for war with Israel. It has amassed a vast arsenal of missiles capable of reaching Israeli territory. It has also armed and funded terrorist proxies like Hezbollah and Hamas on Israel's borders, coinciding with the war preparations described in Ezekiel 38:7.

3. Alliance with Russia

Ezekiel identifies Gog, the leader of the invading forces, as the "prince of Rosh, Meshech, and Tubal" (Ezekiel 38:2), ancient names associated with modern-day Russia. Notably, Russia and Iran have become increasingly close allies in recent years, with their joint military operations in Syria bringing them into close proximity with Israel's northern border. This potentially sets the stage for the prophesied invasion.

4. Positioning in Syria

Iran has taken advantage of the Syrian civil war to establish a military foothold on Israel's doorstep. With Russia's backing, Iran has deployed thousands of troops and built bases in Syria, giving Iran a strategic platform to launch an attack on Israel, just as Ezekiel foretold.

The Divine Orchestration

One of the most striking aspects of Ezekiel's prophecy is the assertion that God Himself will orchestrate and direct this invasion of Israel. The Lord declares,

> "And I will turn you about and put hooks into your jaws, and I will bring you out, and all your army, horses and horsemen, all of them clothed in full armor, a great host, all of them with buckler and shield, wielding swords" (Ezekiel 38:4).

While the nations involved in this alliance may believe they are acting of their own choice, driven by their hatred for Israel or their pursuit of power and resources, the Scripture makes it clear that God is the one who will ultimately provoke and guide them to fulfill His prophetic purposes.

This aspect of the prophecy serves as a powerful reminder that God is in control of human history, and that even the most powerful nations and leaders are mere instruments in His hand. It also underscores the fact that the events unfolding in our world today are not merely the result of human actions but rather are part of a larger, divinely ordained plan.

The Jeremiah Prophecy

In addition to the Gog-Magog prophecy, the book of Jeremiah contains a chilling prediction concerning the fate of Elam, an ancient territory that encompassed parts of modern-day Iran. In Jeremiah 49:34–39, the prophet declares that God will "break the bow of Elam" and bring "disaster upon them, my fierce anger." This prophecy, which has yet to be fulfilled, has led some scholars to speculate that Iran may face divine judgment for its actions against Israel and its defiance of God's purposes.

However, the Jeremiah prophecy ends on a hopeful note: "But in the latter days I will restore the fortunes of Elam, declares the LORD" (Jeremiah 49:39). While the precise meaning of this restoration remains open to interpretation, it suggests that Iran may have a role to play in God's redemptive plan for the nations, even after facing judgment for its actions against Israel.

The Daniel Prophecy

Another intriguing connection between Iran and Bible prophecy can be found in the book of Daniel. In chapter 8, Daniel has a vision of a two-horned ram—representing the Medo-Persian empire—which is eventually defeated by a male goat, symbolizing Greece under Alexander the Great (Daniel 8:20).

While this prophecy was fulfilled in the historical conquest of the Persian Empire by Alexander the Great, some scholars believe that it may also foreshadow a future conflict between Iran and a rising global power, potentially alluding to the Gog-Magog invasion or other end-times event.

The Convergence of Prophecy and Geopolitics

As we examine the remarkable convergence of these prophetic passages with the current geopolitical landscape in the Middle East, it becomes evident that the stage is being set for the fulfillment of these ancient prophecies. The growing tensions between Iran and Israel, coupled with Iran's deepening alliance with Russia and its military build-up in Syria, mirror the prophetic warnings of a future invasion of Israel by a coalition of nations.

The Role of Divine Intervention

While the prophecies concerning Iran's involvement in end-times conflicts paint a dire picture, they also underscore the certainty of God's sovereign intervention. In the Gog-Magog prophecy, God declares that He will intervene to defend Israel and display His power to the nations:

> "With pestilence and bloodshed I will enter into judgment with him, and I will rain upon him and his hordes and the many peoples who are with him torrential rains and hailstones, fire and sulfur" (Ezekiel 38:22).

This divine intervention will ultimately lead to the defeat and destruction of the invading forces, leaving them as plunder for Israel (Ezekiel 39:10) and serving as a powerful testimony of God's sovereignty and unwavering commitment to the preservation of His chosen people (Ezekiel 39:21–22).

The Prophetic Mystery

While the specific details and timing of these prophetic events remain shrouded in mystery, we must approach the study of Bible prophecy with humility and a profound reverence for the sovereignty of God. As believers, we are called to maintain a posture of watchfulness and discernment, seeking wisdom and guidance from God's Word as we try to make sense the complexities of these end-times events.

As we prepare to explore the potential timing of the Gog-Magog War and the escalating tensions surrounding Iran's nuclear program in the chapters that follow, it is crucial to remain anchored in the truth of God's Word and the assurance of His ultimate redemptive plan.

While the path ahead may be fraught with uncertainty and peril, we can take comfort in the knowledge that God is in control, and His divine purposes will ultimately win out. The events unfolding in the Middle East, while often unsettling and complex, are part of a grand plan that has been unfolding since the dawn of human history, culminating in the glorious return of our Lord and Savior, Jesus Christ.

As we bear witness to these prophetic events, let us remain steadfast in our faith, proclaiming the hope and assurance that can only be found in the

God of Abraham, Isaac, and Jacob—the One True God who holds the nations in the palm of His hand. For those who place their trust in Him, these tumultuous events of the last days are not a cause for fear but rather a reminder of the imminent fulfillment of His promises and the establishment of His everlasting Kingdom.

In the next chapter, we will look at the intriguing question of the timing of the Gog-Magog War and explore the potential signs and indicators that may signal the approaching fulfillment of Ezekiel's prophecy. We will examine the biblical clues, historical patterns, and geopolitical developments that could provide insights into when this cataclysmic event may unfold and how it may set the stage for the eventual return of Christ and the ushering in of His eternal reign.

5

Timing Is Everything

In the previous chapter, we explored the prophetic significance of Iran's (Persia's) involvement in the Gog-Magog invasion of Israel, as foretold by the prophet Ezekiel. We investigated the compelling biblical evidence, including the explicit mention of Persia as part of the coalition of nations that will unite against God's chosen people in the latter days. Additionally, we examined other prophetic passages that shed light on Iran's role in the unfolding of end-times events.

As we turn our attention to the timing of this cataclysmic event, it is essential to acknowledge that the precise timing remains a matter of intense debate and speculation among Bible scholars and prophecy experts. While the Scriptures provide us with clues and indicators that can help us understand its potential placement within the broader framework of end-times prophecy, the exact timing remains known only to God.

The Latter Years and the Regathering

One of the most significant clues regarding the timing of the Gog-Magog War is found in Ezekiel 38:8, which states,

> After many days you will be mustered. In the latter years you will go against the land that is restored from war, the land whose people were gathered from many peoples upon the mountains of Israel, which had been a continual waste. Its people were brought out from the peoples and now dwell securely, all of them.

This verse suggests that the Gog-Magog War will occur after the Jewish people have been regathered to their ancient homeland, the land of Israel, and are living in relative security and prosperity. This condition aligns with the current situation in Israel, where the Jewish people have indeed been regathered from various nations and have established a thriving and prosperous nation, albeit surrounded by threats and conflicts.

The Perception of Vulnerability and Peace

Another clue regarding the timing of this prophetic event can be found in Ezekiel 38:10–11, which describes the motivation behind the invasion:

> "Thus says the Lord GOD: On that day, thoughts will come into your mind, and you will devise an

evil scheme and say, 'I will go up against the land of unwalled villages. I will fall upon the quiet people who dwell securely, all of them dwelling without walls, and having no bars or gates.'"

These verses suggests that the invasion will occur when Israel is perceived as vulnerable, without physical defenses or fortifications, indicating a time of relative peace and security within the nation. This condition has not yet been fully realized, as Israel continues to maintain a strong military presence and defensive measures due to the ongoing threats and conflicts in the region.

Four Views on Timing

Among Bible scholars and prophecy experts, there are four main perspectives on the timing of the Gog-Magog War in relation to other end-times events.

View 1: The Pre-Tribulation View
The pre-Tribulation view holds that the invasion will occur before the Rapture of the Church or during the gap between the Rapture and the start of the Tribulation period. Proponents of this view argue that the prophecy depicts Israel as living securely and prosperously, which would be diffi-cult to reconcile with the tumultuous conditions of the Tribulation. Additionally, they contend that the aftermath of the war, with Israel burning the

weapons for seven years (Ezekiel 39:9–10), would not fit within the Tribulation timeline.

Strengths of this view:

- Israel is described as living securely, which aligns with their current state more than the Tribulation period.

- The seven-year burning of weapons doesn't fit well with the timing of the Tribulation.

Weaknesses of this view:

- The prophecy states that the invasion will occur in the "latter years" or "last days," which typically refer to the Tribulation period.

- Israel is not currently dwelling in a state of complete security, as they remain surrounded by hostile neighbors.

View 2: The Early-Tribulation View

Many biblical scholars and prophecy experts believe that the Gog-Magog War will take place during the first half of the seven-year Tribulation period, as described in the book of Revelation. This timeframe would align with the regathering of Israel and the establishment of a temporary peace, potentially facilitated by the Antichrist's covenant with Israel (Daniel 9:27).

Strengths of this view:

- It allows for the seven years of weapons burning to continue through the Tribulation and the seven months of corpse burying to potentially extend into the Millennium.

- It aligns with the idea that the Tribulation will be a period of intense turmoil and conflict, with Israel at the center of the storm.

- The Antichrist's covenant could provide the false sense of security that Israel lacks today.

Weaknesses of this view:

- There is no explicit connection made in Scripture between Ezekiel 38–39 and Daniel's 70th Week (the Tribulation timeframe).

- The aftermath of the war may not fit neatly within the Tribulation timeline.

View 3: The Post-Millennial View

The post-Millennial view proposes that the Gog-Magog War is the same event as the final rebellion against God at the end of the Millennial Kingdom, as described in Revelation 20:8. Proponents of this view point out similarities in language and outcome between Ezekiel 39 and Revelation 20.

Strength of this view:

- The language and outcomes of the two accounts (Ezekiel 39 and Revelation 20) have similarities.

Weaknesses of this view:

- The details of the two accounts differ significantly, suggesting they are separate events.

- The Gog-Magog War is specifically described as occurring in the "latter years," which would not align with the end of the Millennial Kingdom.

- The burial of bodies and burning of weapons would be unnecessary in the transition to the eternal state.

View 4: The Mid-Tribulation View

While not as widely held as the other views, some scholars suggest that the Gog-Magog War could occur around the midpoint of the Tribulation period. According to this view, the defeat of the Gog-Magog coalition by the Lord could pave the way for the Antichrist and his European forces to dominate the world and take over the territory formerly held by Russia and the Islamic states. This would then lead to the Antichrist setting up his world empire and demanding worship in the rebuilt Jewish Temple, triggering the Great Tribulation in the last three and a half years before Christ's return.

Strengths of this view:

- It allows for the seven-year aftermath of the war to fit within the Tribulation and into the Millennium.

- The defeat of the Gog-Magog coalition could create a power vacuum that the Antichrist could exploit to inaugurate his global reign.

Weakness of this view:

- The timing of the invasion at the midpoint of the Tribulation is not explicitly stated in Scripture.

Watchfulness and Discernment

Ultimately, while we can speculate based on the clues provided in Scripture, the precise timing of the Gog-Magog War remains a mystery. As believers, our focus should be on remaining watchful and prepared and faithfully living according to God's Word regardless of when these events unfold.

As we continue to witness the growing tensions and conflicts involving Iran and its allies in the Middle East, it is crucial to keep our eyes fixed on the Scriptures and to remain vigilant, recognizing that the stage is being set for the fulfillment of these ancient prophecies. While the timing may be uncertain, we can rest assured that God's divine plan will unfold according to His perfect will and timing.

In the next chapter, we will look at one of the most pressing and urgent aspects of Iran's prophetic future: its pursuit of nuclear weapons and the implications for Israel and the world. As the Iranian regime continues to defy international sanctions and advance its nuclear program, the specter of a catastrophic confrontation looms large.

We will explore the geopolitical complexities surrounding Iran's nuclear ambitions, the potential consequences of a nuclear-armed Iran, and the various scenarios that could unfold, including the possibility of a preemptive strike by Israel or the United States on Iran's nuclear facilities. Additionally, we will examine the biblical and prophetic implications of a nuclear conflict in the Middle East and how it might align with the unfolding of end-times events.

As we make our way through these turbulent waters, it is essential that we remain anchored in the truth of God's Word and the assurance of His ultimate redemptive plan. While often unsettling and complex, the events unfolding in the Middle East are part of a grand narrative that has been unfolding since the dawn of human history, culminating in the glorious return of our Lord and Savior, Jesus Christ.

6

Nuclear Iran

In the previous chapter, we explored the various perspectives of biblical scholars and prophecy experts concerning the timing of the Gog-Magog War. While the precise timing remains uncertain, one thing is glaringly clear: the escalating tensions between Iran and Israel, fueled by Iran's relentless pursuit of nuclear weapons, have brought the world perilously close to the fulfillment of Ezekiel's chilling prophecy concerning a massive invasion of God's chosen nation.

As we turn our attention to this grave crisis unfolding in the heart of the Middle East, it is crucial that we approach it with a sober understanding of the far-reaching implications, both for regional and global security, as well as for the outworking of biblical prophecy. The specter of a nuclear-armed Iran looms large, casting a dark shadow over the already volatile landscape of the region and raising the terrifying prospect of an apocalyptic conflict that could engulf the world.

The Iranian Nuclear Threat:
A Gathering Storm

Few issues in the realm of geopolitics and international security have garnered as much attention and concern in recent years as Iran's pursuit of nuclear technology. From the outset, the Iranian regime has claimed that its nuclear program is strictly for peaceful energy purposes, but there is ample reason to doubt that claim.

Iran has a long and well-documented history of concealing its uranium enrichment activities from international inspectors, defying calls to halt its nuclear pursuits, and violating the terms of agreements designed to curb its ambitions. The regime's actions have consistently demonstrated a pattern of deception and obfuscation, fueling suspicions that its true intentions are to develop nuclear weapons capabilities.

At the heart of this crisis lies a complex web of historical grievances, ideological differences, and strategic calculations. Iran, a nation with a rich cultural heritage and a deep sense of regional influence, has long viewed its nuclear program as a matter of national pride and a symbol of its technological and scientific prowess. However, the international community, led by the United States and its allies, has repeatedly expressed grave concerns over Iran's nuclear ambitions, fearing that the regime in Tehran is seeking to develop nuclear weapons as a means to project power and further its destabilizing agenda in the region.

These concerns are well-founded. The Iranian regime has made no secret of its unwavering hostility towards Israel, with top officials, including Supreme Leader Ayatollah Ali Khamenei, repeatedly calling for the destruction of the Jewish state. This inflammatory rhetoric, coupled with Iran's support for terrorist organizations like Hezbollah and Hamas, has raised the danger of a regime willing to use nuclear weapons against its perceived enemies, even at the risk of catastrophic retaliation.

Apocalyptic Ideologies and Nuclear Jihad

One of the most alarming aspects of Iran's nuclear ambitions is the role played by the regime's radical Shia Islamic ideology, known as "Twelverism." This belief system holds that the Mahdi, a messianic figure, will return at the end of days amidst a cataclysmic war, ushering in an era of Islamic domination over the world.

Adherents of this ideology, including many within the highest echelons of the Iranian regime, believe that triggering an apocalyptic conflict will hasten the Mahdi's coming and fulfill their religious destiny. This worldview is further reinforced by the regime's messianic fervor and its commitment to exporting its revolutionary Islamist agenda throughout the Middle East and beyond.

In this context, Iran's acquisition of nuclear weapons takes on a terrifying dimension. A nuclear-armed Iran, driven by this apocalyptic worldview, might not be deterred by the threat of retaliation, as its leaders could view a cataclysmic war as a means to fulfill their end-times vision and usher in the return of the Mahdi.

This raises the genuine threat of a "nuclear jihad," a scenario in which Iran uses nuclear weapons against Israel or other perceived enemies, even at the cost of its own destruction. Such a scenario would represent an unprecedented and existential threat to global security, as the world would be forced to grapple with a rogue regime willing to engage in nuclear brinkmanship and potentially unleash unimaginable devastation in pursuit of its ideological objectives.

The Existential Threat to Israel

For Israel, a nuclear-armed Iran represents an existential threat of the highest order. The prospect of a regime that has repeatedly called for Israel's destruction possessing nuclear weapons is a scenario that Israeli policymakers and military planners have long viewed as an unacceptable risk.

Israel has made it abundantly clear that it will not allow Iran to cross the nuclear threshold. The Israeli government, backed by a robust military and intelligence apparatus, has repeatedly warned that it will take whatever action necessary to prevent Iran from acquiring nuclear weapons, including the possibility of preemptive strikes against Iranian nuclear facilities.

Such a move would undoubtedly provoke a fierce response from Iran and its allies, potentially escalating the conflict into a full-blown regional war. Iran has threatened to retaliate against Israel and its allies, and it has also warned that it would attempt to disrupt the global oil supply, which could have severe economic consequences for the entire world.

Moreover, a preemptive strike against Iran's nuclear facilities, while potentially setting back the program, would not necessarily eliminate the threat entirely. Iran's nuclear infrastructure is vast and dispersed, with many facilities buried deep underground or hidden in remote locations, making a comprehensive elimination of its capabilities extremely difficult, if not impossible.

The prospect of a prolonged conflict, involving Iran's extensive network of proxy forces and terrorist organizations, further complicates the strategic calculations for Israel and its allies. Hezbollah, the Iranian-backed militant group based in Lebanon, is believed to possess an arsenal of over 150,000 rockets and missiles, many of which are capable of striking deep into Israeli territory.

A Regional Nuclear Arms Race

Beyond the immediate threat to Israel, a nuclear-armed Iran would also have far-reaching consequences for the broader Middle East region, potentially triggering a nuclear arms race and further destabilizing an already volatile geopolitical landscape.

Many of Iran's regional rivals, including Saudi Arabia, Turkey, and Egypt, have already indicated that they would seek to acquire nuclear weapons as a deterrent against Iranian aggression and to counterbalance Iran's growing influence. Such a scenario would significantly increase the risk of nuclear proliferation and the likelihood of a catastrophic nuclear exchange, either intentional or accidental.

Moreover, a nuclear-armed Iran could embolden the regime to pursue more aggressive and confrontational policies, emboldened by the deterrent effect of its nuclear arsenal. This could lead to increased support for terrorist organizations, further destabilization of neighboring countries, and the potential for direct military confrontation with Israel or other Western powers.

The international community has employed a range of strategies to address the Iranian nuclear issue, including economic sanctions, diplomatic negotiations, and the threat of military action. The Joint Comprehensive Plan of Action (JCPOA), commonly known as the Iran nuclear deal, was a landmark agreement reached in 2015 between Iran and the P5+1 group (the United States, United Kingdom, France, Russia, China, and Germany), designed to curb Iran's nuclear program in exchange for sanctions relief.

However, the fate of the JCPOA has been thrown into uncertainty, with the United States withdrawing from the agreement in 2018 under the Trump administration, citing Iran's continued pursuit of ballistic missile technology and its destabilizing activities in the region. Iran, in turn, has gradually scaled back its commitments in response, enriching uranium to higher levels and accumulating a stockpile that could potentially be used for weapons development.

The Biden administration has expressed a willingness to rejoin the deal, but significant hurdles and disagreements remain, with Iran demanding more concessions and the lifting of all sanctions before it returns to full compliance. The ongoing impasse has only served to heighten tensions and increase the likelihood of a military confrontation, either through a preemptive strike by Israel on Iran's nuclear facilities or a miscalculation that could spiral out of control.

Prophetic Implications: The Gog-Magog Scenario

As we grapple with the complexities of the Iranian nuclear crisis, it is imperative that we approach the issue not only from a geopolitical and strategic perspective but also through the lens of biblical prophecy. The potential involvement of Iran in the prophesied Gog-Magog invasion of Israel, as foretold by the prophet Ezekiel, adds a profound layer of significance to the current crisis and raises the stakes to an unprecedented level.

The implications of Ezekiel chapters 38 and 39 are profound, as they suggest that Iran will play a central role in a future conflict that will pit a coalition of nations against Israel. This prophecy has taken on increased significance in recent years, as Iran's pursuit of nuclear weapons and its unwavering hostility towards Israel have raised the stakes.

Ezekiel's prophecy provides a remarkable glimpse into the geopolitical landscape of the last days, with several key details aligning with the current realities in the Middle East:

1. Iran's Hostility Toward Israel

Since the 1979 Islamic Revolution, Iran's leaders have repeatedly called for Israel's destruction. They refer to Israel as the "Little Satan" and a "cancerous tumor" that needs to be eradicated. This seething hatred will culminate in Iran's enthusiastic participation in the prophesied invasion of Israel.

2. Military Preparations

Iran has been actively preparing for war with Israel. It has amassed a vast arsenal of missiles capable of reaching Israeli territory, and it has also armed and funded terrorist proxies like Hezbollah and Hamas on Israel's borders, coinciding with the war preparations described in Ezekiel 38:7. Although Israel and its allies successfully thwarted a missile and drone attack on April 13, 2024, there's no reason to believe Iran isn't already adjusting its military strategy.

3. The Alliance with Russia

Ezekiel identifies Gog, the leader of the invading forces, as the "prince of Rosh, Meshech, and Tubal" (Ezekiel 38:2). Rosh is associated with modern-day Russia. Notably, Russia and Iran have become increasingly close allies in recent years, with their joint military operations in Syria bringing them into close proximity with Israel's northern border, potentially setting the stage for the prophesied invasion.

4. Positioning in Syria

Iran has taken advantage of the Syrian civil war to establish a military foothold on Israel's doorstep. With Russia's backing, Iran has deployed thousands of troops and built bases in Syria, giving them a strategic platform to launch an attack on Israel, just as Ezekiel foretold. Israel's alleged attack on April 1, 2024, on the Iranian consulate is in response to this threat.

The prospect of a nuclear-armed Iran fits disturbingly well with the Gog-Magog scenario. In this prophetic event, Iran and its allies will launch an all-out attack on Israel, which could potentially involve the use of weapons of mass destruction, including nuclear arms. The severity of the battle, with God's supernatural intervention wiping out the invading armies through "a torrential rain, hailstones, fire, and brimstone" (Ezekiel 38:22 NASB), suggests a level of devastation consistent with nuclear warfare.

While we cannot be certain of the specific details, Iran's aggressive nuclear program and apocalyptic ideology are setting the stage for a catastrophic end-times conflict. The prospect of a regime driven by messianic fervor and a willingness to engage in nuclear maneuvering raises the terrifying possibility of a scenario that could unfold in a manner consistent with Ezekiel's prophecy.

Aftermath and Restoration

Beyond the climactic confrontation foretold in the Gog-Magog prophecy, the Scriptures also provide glimpses into the potential aftermath and restoration that may follow. Ezekiel's prophecy describes a period during which Israel will be occupied for seven months with burying the dead and seven years with burning the weapons of the defeated invaders (Ezekiel 39:9–10, 14).

This extended period of cleanup and restoration suggests that the aftermath of this conflict will be of unprecedented scale and severity, requiring a concerted effort by Israel and potentially the international community to recover from the devastation.

Moreover, the prophet Jeremiah's reference to the restoration of Elam (modern-day Iran) in the "latter days" (Jeremiah 49:39) suggests that even after facing divine judgment for its actions against Israel, Iran may have a role to play in God's redemptive plan for humanity.

While the precise meaning of this restoration remains open to interpretation, it raises the possibility of a future reconciliation between Israel and Iran, or perhaps even the salvation of the Iranian people and their embrace of the God of Abraham, Isaac, and Jacob.

Navigating the Path Ahead

As we consider the complexities of the Iranian nuclear crisis and the potential fulfillment of Ezekiel's Gog-Magog prophecy, it is essential for believers to maintain a posture of watchfulness, discernment, and steadfast faith.

While the prospect of a nuclear-armed Iran is undoubtedly a cause for grave concern, our ultimate hope and trust must lie in the sovereign plan of God, who has foretold the ultimate triumph of His purposes in the face of even the most daunting challenges. The road ahead will be fraught with challenges and uncertainties, but we can take comfort in the knowledge that God is in control and that His divine plan will prevail.

As we witness the unfolding of these momentous events, let us remain anchored in the truth of God's Word and the assurance of His redemptive plan for humanity. Let us pray for the salvation of the Iranian people and for the leaders of nations to have wisdom and discernment in navigating this volatile situation.

And above all, let us hold fast to the promises of God, knowing that no matter how dire the circumstances, He will protect His people and fulfill His purposes in the last days, ushering in the glorious return of our Lord and Savior, Jesus Christ.

In the next chapter, we will look even closer at a gripping and detailed account of the prophesied Gog-Magog War, drawing upon the vivid descriptions found in Ezekiel's prophecy. We will explore the unfolding of this cataclysmic event, the divine intervention that will bring about the defeat of the invading forces, and the aftermath that will follow in the wake of this monumental conflict.

As we explore these profound prophecies, we will gain a deeper understanding of the role that Iran and its allies will play in this end-times scenario, as well as the broader implications for Israel and the nations of the world. Through this exploration, we will be better equipped to discern the signs of the times and prepare ourselves for the momentous events that lie ahead, all while resting in the assurance of God's sovereign plan and ultimate victory over the forces of darkness.

The Gog-Magog War

In the previous chapter, we explored the grave threat posed by a nuclear-armed Iran and the potential for an apocalyptic conflict with Israel, aligning disturbingly well with the prophesied Gog-Magog invasion foretold in Ezekiel's prophecy. As we navigate these turbulent waters, it is crucial that we turn our attention to the vivid and chilling account provided by the prophet himself, shedding light on the unfolding of this cataclysmic event, God's divine intervention, and the profound aftermath that will reshape the geopolitical landscape.

The Invasion Foretold

According to the prophecy recorded in Ezekiel chapters 38 and 39, a vast coalition of nations, led by the enigmatic figure of "Gog, of the land of Magog," will launch a massive invasion against the land of Israel. This formidable alliance, comprising nations such as Russia (Rosh), Magog (central Asian nations), Persia (modern-day Iran), Cush (Sudan), Put (Libya), Gomer, Meshach, and Tubal (Turkey), and Beth-togarmah (possibly regions of modern-day Turkey, Armenia, and Turkmenistan), will descend upon Israel like a storm, covering the land like a cloud (Ezekiel 38:9, 16).

The motivations behind this invasion are chillingly straightforward: greed and a desire for conquest. Ezekiel 38:10–12 reveals that the invading forces will seek to plunder the wealth and resources of a prosperous and seemingly defenseless Israel, dwelling in "unwalled villages" and perceiving itself to be secure. The prophet's description paints a picture of a nation caught off guard, unprepared for the onslaught that is about to befall it.

The Gathering Storm

As the stage is set for this prophetic invasion, the prophet provides further details about the composition and strength of the invading forces. Ezekiel 38:4 describes the coalition as "a great host, all of them with buckler and shield, wielding swords." This vivid imagery suggests a formidable military might, equipped with the weapons and armor of war, all poised to descend upon the land of Israel like a relentless storm.

The prophet's account also hints at the strategic positioning of these forces, with Ezekiel 38:6 describing the invaders as coming "from the uttermost parts of the north." This detail aligns with the geographical locations of nations like Russia and Turkey, situated to the north of Israel, further solidifying the interpretation of Gog's coalition as a modern-day alliance of nations from the regions of the former Soviet Union and the Middle East.

At the Brink of Annihilation

As the invasion unfolds, the prophet paints a harrowing picture of Israel's dire circumstances. Militarily, the tiny nation will be completely outnumbered and surrounded by the combined might of the Russian-Islamic coalition. Defeat and destruction will appear certain, leaving Israel on the brink of annihilation.

Ezekiel's prophecy emphasizes the sense of vulnerability and perceived defenselessness of Israel, describing the nation as dwelling "without walls" (Ezekiel 38:11). This detail is significant, as it suggests a time when Israel will be lulled into a false sense of security, perhaps as a result of a temporary peace treaty or agreement facilitated by the Antichrist, as foretold in Daniel 9:27.

The prophet's words echo the sentiments of the invading forces:

> "Thus says the Lord GOD: On that day, thoughts will come into your mind, and you will devise an evil scheme and say, 'I will go up against the land of unwalled villages. I will fall upon the quiet people who dwell securely, all of them dwelling without walls, and having no bars or gates'" (Ezekiel 38:10–11).

This perception of Israel's vulnerability will serve as the catalyst for the attack, as the coalition sees an opportunity to strike at a seemingly defenseless target.

But it is at this moment of seeming triumph for the enemy that God's intervention will be revealed in all its glory.

Divine Intervention and Judgment

"I will summon a sword against Gog on all my mountains, declares the Lord GOD. Every man's sword will be against his brother. With pestilence and bloodshed I will enter into judgment with him, and I will rain upon him and his hordes and the many peoples who are with him torrential rains and hailstones, fire and sulfur. So I will show my greatness and my holiness and make myself known in the eyes of many nations. Then they will know that I am the LORD (Ezekiel 38:21–23).

God will unleash a series of catastrophic judgments upon the invading forces. The earth itself will tremble under the weight of God's wrath, as a mighty earthquake rocks the land of Israel, throwing the invaders into panic and confusion (Ezekiel 38:19–20).

In the midst of this chaos, the Lord will turn the invading soldiers against one another, causing them to descend into infighting and slaughter among their own ranks (Ezekiel 38:21). The judgments will intensify, with God raining down pestilence, bloodshed, torrential rains, hailstones, and even fire from the heavens upon the enemy forces, utterly decimating them (Ezekiel 38:22).

The prophet's account leaves no doubt as to the supernatural nature of this intervention, with God employing cosmic disturbances and unleashing the very elements against the invaders. Ezekiel 38:19 describes God's "blazing wrath" being poured out "with pestilence and bloodshed" (v. 22), suggesting the possibility of biological or even nuclear contamination ravaging the enemy forces.

The descriptive language used by the prophet is both vivid and terrifying, with references to "torrential rains and hailstones, fire and sulfur" (Ezekiel 38:22). These details evoke images of cataclysmic natural disasters and cosmic upheavals, all serving as instruments of God's judgment upon the invading armies.

A Testimony to God's Power

The aftermath of this divine intervention will be nothing short of awe-inspiring, a powerful demonstration of God's sovereignty and might. The Lord declares,

> "So I will show my greatness and my holiness and make myself known in the eyes of many nations. Then they will know that I am the LORD" (Ezekiel 38:23).

The sheer magnitude of God's victory will be a testimony to His power, leaving no room for doubt or disbelief. The nations of the world will be forced to acknowledge the supremacy of the Almighty, and the fear of the Lord will fall upon the surrounding peoples (Ezekiel 38:20).

The prophet's words echo the sentiments of God's declaration in Ezekiel 39:7:

> "And my holy name I will make known in the midst
> of my people Israel, and I will not let my holy name be
> profaned anymore. And the nations shall know that I
> am the LORD, the Holy One in Israel."

This revelation of God's sovereignty and holiness will serve as a powerful witness to the nations, shattering their idolatrous beliefs and false ideologies and ushering in a recognition of the One True God.

The Scale of Destruction

The prophet's account leaves no doubt as to the scale of the destruction wrought upon the invading forces. Ezekiel describes the grim task of burying the dead, which will take seven months to complete (Ezekiel 39:12–13). The slain invaders will litter the mountains of Israel, providing a grotesque feast for carrion birds and beasts (Ezekiel 39:4–5, 17–20).

The prophet's language is graphic and unflinching, painting a vivid picture of the carnage that will ensue. Ezekiel 39:11 describes "the Valley of the Travelers, east of the sea," where the invading forces will be buried, a grim reminder of the magnitude of their defeat.

Moreover, the judgment will extend beyond the battlefield, with the Lord declaring,

> "I will send fire on Magog and on those who dwell
> securely in the coastlands, and they shall know that I
> am the LORD" (Ezekiel 39:6).

This chilling pronouncement suggests that the homelands of the invading nations, including Russia and its distant territories, will also experience devastating destruction, crippling their power and influence on the global stage.

The Cleansing and Restoration of Israel

In the wake of this monumental victory, the Lord promises to restore the fortunes of Israel and to gather His people from the nations where they have been scattered (Ezekiel 39:25–29). This restoration will be a fulfillment of God's covenant with His chosen people and a demonstration of His faithfulness to His promises.

The prophet's account emphasizes the need for a thorough cleansing of the land, with the people of Israel spending seven years gathering and burning the weapons of the defeated invaders (Ezekiel 39:9–10). This extended period of cleansing and purification will serve as a symbolic act of renewal and preparation for the next phase of God's redemptive plan.

For Israel, the Gog-Magog War will be a turning point, as God declares,

> "The house of Israel shall know that I am the LORD their God, from that day forward" (Ezekiel 39:22).

The Jewish people, having witnessed the miraculous intervention of the Almighty, will finally embrace their Messiah, ushering in a new era of spiritual awakening and recognition of the One True God.

The prophet's words echo the sentiments expressed in Zechariah 12:10:

> "And I will pour out on the house of David and the inhabitants of Jerusalem a spirit of grace and pleas for mercy, so that, when they look on me, on him whom they have pierced, they shall mourn for him, as one mourns for an only child, and weep bitterly over him, as one weeps over a firstborn."

This spiritual revival among the Jewish people will pave the way for the establishment of the Millennial Kingdom, where Christ will reign as the rightful King and the nations will come to worship Him in Jerusalem (Zechariah 14:16–19).

The Geopolitical Landscape Transformed

The aftermath of the Gog-Magog War will also have profound geopolitical implications, reshaping the balance of power in the Middle East and potentially paving the way for the rise of the Antichrist and his global empire.

With the Russian-Islamic alliance decimated, the Western powers, led by the Antichrist, may seize the opportunity to fill the power vacuum left in the region, consolidating their control over the Middle East and its resources, particularly oil. Having defeated the armies of the East, the Antichrist could rapidly consolidate his global empire and demand the world's worship, ushering in the most terrible phase of the Tribulation.

The prophet Daniel provides further insights into this geopolitical shift:

> And the king shall do as he wills. He shall exalt himself and magnify himself above every god, and shall speak astonishing things against the God of gods (Daniel 11:36).

This "king," believed to be the Antichrist, will establish his dominion over the earth, setting the stage for the final confrontation between the forces of good and evil.

The Role of the Antichrist

As the dust settles from the Gog-Magog War, the Antichrist will seize the opportunity to establish his global empire. The prophet Daniel describes this figure as "a king of bold face, one who understands riddles" (Daniel 8:23). He will be a master of intrigue, skilled in deception and manipulation.

The Antichrist will exploit the power vacuum left by the decimation of the Russian-Islamic coalition, positioning himself to the rule the world. This will mark the beginning of the Great Tribulation, a period of unparalleled suffering and turmoil that will culminate in the Battle of Armageddon and the glorious Second Coming of Christ.

God will not abandon Israel nor allow her enemies to triumph in the end. His divine plan will prevail, and His glory will be revealed to all nations, just as foretold by the prophet Ezekiel.

Throughout these tumultuous events, God's hand will be evident, orchestrating the affairs of nations and individuals to bring about the fulfillment of His purposes. The prophet Ezekiel repeatedly emphasizes this truth, declaring,

> "So I will show my greatness and my holiness and make myself known in the eyes of many nations. Then they will know that I am the LORD" (Ezekiel 38:23).

Preparing for the Unfolding of Prophecy

As we contemplate the unfolding of these prophetic events, we must recognize that the Gog-Magog War, while a decisive victory for Israel, is not the end of her troubles. It is but one stage in the unfolding of God's end-times plan, which will culminate in the return of Christ and the establishment of His Millennial Kingdom.

In the next chapter, we will explore the reasons why the stage is set for the Gog-Magog War and other end-times events, taking a look at the convergence of geopolitical, cultural, and technological developments that align with biblical prophecy. We will examine the significance of Israel's rebirth as a nation, the rise of globalism, and the technological advancements that may pave the way for the fulfillment of ancient prophecies.

8

The Stage Is Set

In the previous chapter, we explored the vivid and chilling account of the Gog-Magog War as foretold by the prophet Ezekiel. We witnessed the unfolding of this cataclysmic event, the divine intervention that will bring about the defeat of the invading forces, and the profound aftermath that will reshape the geopolitical landscape. As we emerge from this prophetic narrative, we are confronted with a sobering reality: the stage is rapidly being set for the fulfillment of these ancient prophecies and other end-times events.

The Convergence of Prophetic Signs

As we survey the geopolitical scene today, a remarkable convergence of factors indicates that we are indeed living in the last days and that the return of Christ is drawing near. These signs align with biblical prophecies in a way that would have been unimaginable just a few decades ago, compelling us to take heed and be watchful.

The Regathering of Israel

One of the most significant signs is the regathering of the Jewish people to their ancient homeland, a prerequisite for the fulfillment of end-times prophecies. The modern State of Israel, established in 1948, is a miraculous actualization of God's promise to bring His people back from exile (Ezekiel 36:24; Isaiah 11:11–12). This restoration of Israel sets the stage for the events described in Scripture, including the Gog-Magog War.

For centuries, the Jewish people were scattered across the globe, persecuted, and driven from their homeland. Yet in fulfillment of countless biblical prophecies, they have returned to the land promised to their forefathers, Abraham, Isaac, and Jacob. This remarkable feat, achieved against overwhelming odds and opposition, stands as a testament to the faithfulness of God and the reliability of His Word.

The Alignment of Nations Against Israel

Ezekiel's prophecy foretold the formation of an alliance between nations such as Russia, Iran, Turkey, and others, united in their hostility toward Israel. Today, we are witnessing the deepening military and economic ties between these countries, particularly in Syria, providing a clear staging ground for the prophesied invasion. Moreover, the increasing worldwide animosity toward Israel and the Jewish people, fueled by anti-Semitism and delegitimization efforts, aligns with prophecies such as

Zechariah 12:2–3 and 14:2, which foretell a global conflict centered on Jerusalem during the Tribulation period.

The growing influence of radical Islam and the rise of terrorist organizations like Hamas, Hezbollah, and ISIS have fueled the hatred toward Israel and the Jewish people. These groups, backed by nations like Iran, have made no secrct of their desire to wipe Israel off the map, echoing the sentiments expressed in Psalm 83:4: "Come, let us wipe them out as a nation; let the name of Israel be remembered no more!"

The Rise of Globalism and the March Toward a One-World System

The push for a global system, politically, economically, and religiously, resonates with the prophecies concerning the rise of the Antichrist and the establishment of a one-world government. The book of Revelation speaks of a one-world system under the Antichrist, where technology will be used to control and monitor humanity through means such as the Mark of the Beast (Revelation 13:16–17).

We see this trend toward globalism manifesting in various forms, from the rise of multinational corporations and global governance bodies like the United Nations, to the push for a unified currency and the erosion of national sovereignty. The COVID-19 pandemic has further accelerated this trend, as governments around the world have implemented unprecedented measures to control and monitor their populations, setting the stage for a potential global system of control and surveillance.

The Acceleration of Moral Decay and Rejection of Biblical Values

The moral and spiritual decline of our world, marked by increasing violence, wickedness, and the celebration of ungodliness, mirrors the signs foretold by Jesus and the apostles concerning the state of the world in the last days (Matthew 24:37–39; 2 Timothy 3:1–5; 2 Thessalonians 2:3).

We live in a time when traditional values and moral absolutes are being systematically eroded, replaced by a culture of relativism and self-gratification. The sanctity of life, the institution of marriage, and the very concept of gender are under assault, while the pursuit of pleasure and personal fulfillment reigns supreme.

This moral decay is not limited to secular society but has also infiltrated the Church, with many professing believers embracing worldly philosophies and compromising biblical truth. Here is the apostle Paul's warning to Timothy about people in the last days:

> For the time is coming when people will not endure sound teaching, but having itching ears they will accumulate for themselves teachers to suit their own passions, and will turn away from listening to the truth and wander off into myths (2 Timothy 4:3–4).

This description has become the sobering reality of our present day.

The Proliferation of Technology and Advancements in Artificial Intelligence

The rapid advancement of technology, including artificial intelligence (AI), bioengineering, and surveillance systems, could facilitate the end-times scenario described in Scripture, paving the way for the Antichrist's control over the global economy and the implementation of the Mark of the Beast system.

We live in an era where technology has become deeply intertwined with every aspect of our lives, from commerce and communication to entertainment and transportation. The rise of smart devices, biometric identification, and digital currencies has set the stage for a global system of control and monitoring that was once unimaginable.

Furthermore, the development of AI and biotechnology has raised ethical and existential questions about the very nature of humanity. The pursuit of transhumanism, the merging of human beings with technology, has become a reality, blurring the lines between the natural and the artificial.

The Destabilization of the Middle East and the Rise of Radical Islam

The chaos and instability in the Middle East, fueled by the rise of radical Islamic groups like ISIS and the Muslim Brotherhood, have created a vacuum for new alliances to form, aligning with Ezekiel's prophecy concerning the nations that will unite against Israel.

The so-called Arab Spring, which began with promises of democracy and freedom, quickly devolved into a series of civil wars, power struggles, and the rise of extremist groups. Nations like Syria, Libya, and Yemen have descended into chaos, providing fertile ground for terrorist organizations to take root and spread their ideology of hate and violence.

This instability has also allowed nations like Iran and Turkey to assert their influence in the region, form strategic alliances, and position themselves as key players in the unfolding of end-times events.

The Apostasy and Deception in the Church
The growing prevalence of false teachings, doctrines of demons, and the departure from biblical truth within the Church mirrors the warnings of Jesus and the apostles concerning the apostasy that will characterize the last days (Matthew 24:11–12; 2 Thessalonians 2:3; 1 Timothy 4:1).

In our time, we have witnessed the rise of new age spirituality and the acceptance of unbiblical ideologies within the Church. Many professing believers have embraced cultural trends and philosophies that are diametrically opposed to the teachings of Scripture, leading to a watering down of the gospel and a distortion of biblical truth.

This apostasy has not only created confusion and division within the body of Christ but has also weakened the Church's witness to the world. As believers compromise their convictions and conform to the patterns of this world, the salt has lost its savor, and the light has grown dim.

The Rise of Global Communication

With the advent of modern technology, including satellite TV, the internet, and social media, the gospel message is being shared with the world like never before in history. While the Church has faced persecution and opposition throughout its history, the age of global communication has opened new doors for the spread of the gospel. Missionaries, evangelists, and believers from all walks of life are leveraging technology to reach the uttermost parts of the earth with the Good News of Jesus Christ.

This global evangelistic effort, coupled with the persecution and suffering of believers in many parts of the world, is a clear sign that we are living in the last days and that the return of Christ is drawing near.

The Acceleration of End-Times Indicators

While these signs and developments are not new, their convergence and acceleration in recent years are unprecedented. We do not see some of the signs; we are witnessing *all* of the signs. It is as if the final pieces of a prophetic puzzle are rapidly falling into place, aligning with biblical prophecies in a way that was previously unimaginable.

The COVID-19 pandemic, though not necessarily a specific fulfillment of prophecy, has nevertheless exposed the vulnerability of our global systems and demonstrated how quickly the world can be brought to a standstill. It has also illustrated the readiness of people to accept government control and restrictions, setting the stage for the potential rise of a global leader who promises security and stability.

Moreover, the increasing frequency and intensity of natural disasters, environmental crises, and geopolitical tensions point toward the biblical descriptions of the "birth pangs" that will precede the return of Christ and the establishment of His Millennial Kingdom (Matthew 24:8).

Jesus likened these events to the labor pains of a pregnant woman, indicating that they would increase in frequency and intensity as the time of His return draws near. Just as a woman's contractions become more frequent and intense as the birth draws closer, so too will the world experience an escalation of calamities and upheavals as the end-times approach.

We have witnessed this phenomenon in recent years, with unprecedented natural disasters such as hurricanes, earthquakes, and wildfires ravaging various parts of the globe. Additionally, the threat of global pandemics, climate change, and the proliferation of weapons of mass destruction have added to the sense of unease and instability that permeates our world.

While these events are not necessarily prophetic in themselves, they serve as stark reminders of the fragility of our existence and the need for a Savior. They also align with the biblical descriptions of the conditions that will characterize the end-times, further underscoring the urgency of the hour in which we live.

The Perspective of the Prophets

As we traverse these momentous events, we must consider the perspective of the prophets who foretold these things centuries ago. The apostle Peter, writing to the scattered believers of his day, encouraged them to "count the patience of our Lord as salvation" (2 Peter 3:15). He reminded them that the Lord is not slow in keeping His promise, but is patient, desiring that all should come to repentance (2 Peter 3:9).

Similarly, the prophet Habakkuk, in the midst of foretelling the impending judgment of God upon the nations, expressed his trust in the Lord's sovereign plan:

> Though the fig tree should not blossom,
>   nor fruit be on the vines,
> the produce of the olive fail
>   and the fields yield no food,
> the flock be cut off from the fold
>   and there be no herd in the stalls,

yet I will rejoice in the LORD;
  I will take joy in the God of my salvation
    (Habakkuk 3:17–18).

These prophets understood that the unfolding of God's plan, while often accompanied by turmoil and upheaval, was ultimately leading to the redemption of humanity and the establishment of His eternal Kingdom. They recognized that the trials and tribulations of their day were but birth pangs, heralding the coming of a new era of peace and righteousness under the reign of the Messiah.

As we witness the convergence of prophetic signs and the acceleration of end-times indicators, we must embrace this same perspective. While the world around us may be in chaos, we can find comfort and hope in the knowledge that God's purposes are being fulfilled and that the ultimate triumph of His Kingdom is assured.

The Testimony of the Church

Throughout the ages, the Church has been a witness to the unfolding of God's redemptive plan. From the persecutions of the early believers to the great revivals and missions movements, the body of Christ has played a pivotal role in the proclamation of the Gospel and the preparation for the return of the Lord.

In our day, the Church has a unique opportunity and responsibility to bear witness to the convergence of prophetic signs and the imminent return of Christ. As the world descends into chaos and darkness, the light of the gospel must shine brighter than ever before.

The apostle Paul, in his letter to the Philippians, exhorted believers this way:

> Do all things without grumbling or disputing, that you may be blameless and innocent, children of God without blemish in the midst of a crooked and twisted generation, among whom you shine as lights in the world, holding fast to the word of life, so that in the day of Christ I may be proud that I did not run in vain or labor in vain (Philippians 2:14–16).

As the end-times draw near, the Church must be a beacon of hope and truth, proclaiming the Good News of salvation and pointing the way to the only source of true peace and security: Jesus Christ.

Moreover, the Church must be a voice of reason and clarity amidst the confusion and deception that will characterize the last days. Jesus warned of the rise of false prophets and false messiahs, who would seek to lead people astray (Matthew 24:24). It is incumbent upon the body of Christ to be well-grounded in the truth of God's Word, discerning the times and exposing the lies of the enemy.

The Church must also be a place of refuge and support for those who are suffering and persecuted for their faith. As the world becomes increasingly hostile to Christianity, believers will need a strong, united, and loving community to provide encouragement, prayer, and practical assistance.

Furthermore, the Church must be a model of unity, transcending ethnic, cultural, and denominational barriers. As the end-times approach, the body of Christ must come together in a spirit of love and cooperation, setting aside petty differences and focusing on the common goal of proclaiming the gospel and preparing for the return of the Lord.

The apostle Paul's exhortation to the Ephesian church is particularly relevant in our day:

> I therefore, a prisoner for the Lord, urge you to walk in a manner worthy of the calling to which you have been called, with all humility and gentleness, with patience, bearing with one another in love, eager to maintain the unity of the Spirit in the bond of peace (Ephesians 4:1-3).

As the Church experiences the challenges and opportunities of the end-times, it must remain faithful to its calling, proclaiming the truth of the gospel, standing firm in the face of opposition, and eagerly awaiting the return of its Savior and King.

The Certainty of God's Promises

Amid the turmoil and uncertainty of our times, we can find comfort and assurance in the certainty of God's promises. Throughout the ages, the Lord has faithfully fulfilled His Word, and He will not fail to bring to pass the ultimate triumph of His Kingdom.

The prophet Isaiah declared,

> A voice says, "Cry!"
>   And I said, "What shall I cry?"
> All flesh is grass,
>   and all its beauty is like the flower of the
>   field.
> The grass withers, the flower fades
>   when the breath of the LORD blows on it;
>   surely the people are grass.
> The grass withers, the flower fades,
>   but the word of our God will stand forever
>   (Isaiah 40:6–8).

God's promises are eternal and unchanging, and they will be fulfilled in their appointed time.

As we witness the unfolding of prophetic events and the convergence of signs pointing to the imminence of Christ's return, we can cling to the promise of the Lord Jesus Himself:

> "Heaven and earth will pass away, but my words will not pass away" (Matthew 24:35).

The apostle Peter, writing to the believers of his day, encouraged them:

> Therefore, preparing your minds for action, and being sober-minded, set your hope fully on the grace that will be brought to you at the revelation of Jesus Christ (1 Peter 1:13).

The trials and tribulations we may face are but birth pangs, heralding the imminent return of our Lord and the establishment of His eternal Kingdom.

As we prepare to consider the practical implications of living in these last days, let us also embrace the words of the apostle John:

> Beloved, we are God's children now, and what we will be has not yet appeared; but we know that when he appears we shall be like him, because we shall see him as he is. And everyone who thus hopes in him purifies himself as he is pure (1 John 3:2–3).

May this hope, this blessed assurance, fill our hearts and guide our steps as we walk through the challenges and opportunities of these end-times. Though the world may tremble and the nations rage, our God reigns supreme, and His purposes will ultimately prevail.

Conclusion

Living in Dangerous Times

As we come to the end of this journey through the prophetic destiny of Iran and Israel, we have explored a sobering reality—the signs of the times are converging, and the stage is being set for the fulfillment of biblical prophecies concerning the endtimes. From the escalating tensions between Iran and Israel to the broader geopolitical landscape, we have witnessed a remarkable alignment of events that echo the ancient words of the prophets.

In **Chapter 1,** we examined the prophetic significance of the nations that will unite against Israel in the Gog-Magog invasion, as foretold by the prophet Ezekiel. We examined the key players, including Russia, Iran, Turkey, and others, and how their deepening alliances and positioning in the Middle East align with the biblical narrative.

Chapter 2 took us on a journey through the rich tapestry of Iran's interactions with the people of God throughout Scripture, from its formative role in the restoration of Jerusalem to the symbolic prophecies concerning its rise and fall. We explored the profound significance of Persia (Iran) in the out-working of God's redemptive plan.

In **Chapter 3,** we traced the turbulent history of Iran, from the glory days of the Persian Empire to the tumultuous events of the Islamic Revolution and the contemporary era. We uncovered the cultural, religious, and political forces that have shaped Iran's contemporary worldview and positioned it as a leading adversary of Israel and the West.

Chapter 4 took a deeper dive into the heart of biblical prophecy, unveiling the central role of Iran in the prophesied Gog-Magog invasion of Israel. We explored the chilling details of Ezekiel's prophecy, the alignment of current events with the scriptural narrative, and the potential for divine intervention and judgment.

In **Chapter 5,** we grappled with the complex question of timing, examining the various perspectives on when the Gog-Magog War might occur in relation to other end-times events, such as the Tribulation period and the rise of the Antichrist.

Chapter 6 confronted the grave threat posed by a nuclear-armed Iran, exploring the apocalyptic ideologies that drive the regime's pursuit of atomic weapons and the existential danger this poses to Israel and the world.

Chapter 7 provided a vivid and chilling account of the Gog-Magog War itself, drawing upon the prophetic descriptions found in Ezekiel's writings. We learned about the unfolding of this cataclysmic event, God's divine intervention, and the profound aftermath that will reshape the geopolitical landscape.

In **Chapter 8,** we explored the reasons why the stage is set for the Gog-Magog War and other end-times events, examining the convergence of geopolitical, cultural, and technological developments that align with Bible prophecy.

As we stand at the culmination of this prophetic journey, the question that weighs heavily upon our hearts is this: ***How should we, as Christians, live in these dangerous times?***

The Urgency of the Hour

The imminent return of Christ demands a response from every believer, compelling us to live with vigilance, purpose, and a sense of expectancy. The signs of the times should not instill fear or despair in us but should instead serve as a serious call to pursue holiness, purity, and a deeper relationship with our Lord through prayer and devotion.

The imminence of Christ's return should motivate us to examine our lives, confess our sins, and walk in obedience to God's Word, ensuring that our hearts are firmly rooted in His truth.

Proclaiming the Gospel

In these perilous times, we must be diligent in sharing the gospel message with those who are lost and perishing. As the world descends into chaos and darkness, the light of Christ will shine even brighter, and we have a sacred obligation to proclaim the Good News while there is still time.

Jesus Himself commanded His disciples to "go into all the world and proclaim the gospel to the whole creation" (Mark 16:15). This Great Commission has taken on a renewed urgency in our day, as we see the signs of His return manifesting around us. We must be bold and courageous in our witness, seizing every opportunity to share the love and truth of Christ with those who are lost.

The apostle Paul's exhortation resonates with renewed significance:

> Walk in wisdom toward outsiders, making the best use of the time. Let your speech always be gracious, seasoned with salt, so that you may know how you ought to answer each person (Colossians 4:5–6).

As the end draws near, our words and actions must reflect the urgency of the hour, pointing people to the only source of true hope and salvation: Jesus Christ.

Standing Firm in the Face of Turmoil and Persecution

In the face of the world's turmoil and the imminent return of Christ, we must live with an eternal perspective, investing our time, talents, and resources into that which has eternal value. The things of this world are passing away, but God's Kingdom will endure forever.

The apostle Paul exhorted the Corinthian believers, saying,

> So we do not lose heart. Though our outer self is wasting away, our inner self is being renewed day by day. For this light momentary affliction is preparing for us an eternal weight of glory beyond all comparison, as we look not to the things that are seen but to the things that are unseen. For the things that are seen are transient, but the things that are unseen are eternal (2 Corinthians 4:16–18).

As we witness the unfolding of end-times events, we must keep our eyes fixed on the eternal realities that await us, investing our lives in that which will endure for eternity.

This eternal perspective should shape our priorities, our use of resources, and our daily decisions. We must store up treasures in Heaven rather than on earth, using our gifts to serve the body of Christ, supporting ministries that advance the gospel, and being generous toward those in need (Matthew 6:19–20).

We must remember that our true citizenship is in Heaven and that this world is not our permanent home. The apostle Paul exhorted the Philippians,

> But our citizenship is in heaven, and from it we await a Savior, the Lord Jesus Christ, who will transform our

lowly body to be like his glorious body, by the power
that enables him even to subject all things to himself
(Philippians 3:20–21).

We must set our minds on things above, not on
earthly things (Colossians 3:2) and live as strangers
and exiles in this world, looking forward to the city
that is to come (Hebrews 11:13–16).

As we ponder the complexities of these end-
times, it is essential that we maintain a posture of
watchfulness and discernment, seeking wisdom and
guidance from the Scriptures and remaining vigilant
for the signs of Christ's imminent return. While we
cannot know the exact day or hour, we must heed
the words of Jesus, who exhorted His disciples:

"Therefore, stay awake, for you do not know on what
day your Lord is coming" (Matthew 24:42).

As the world becomes increasingly hostile to biblical
values and the message of the gospel, we must stand
firm in our faith, even in the face of persecution and
adversity. The apostle Peter, writing to believers who
were facing intense persecution, encouraged them:

But rejoice insofar as you share Christ's sufferings,
that you may also rejoice and be glad when his glory
is revealed (1 Peter 4:13).

We must be prepared to endure hardship and
opposition for the sake of the gospel, knowing that

our reward is eternal and that our suffering is but temporary. The words of Jesus should resonate in our hearts:

> "Blessed are you when people hate you and when they exclude you and revile you and spurn your name as evil, on account of the Son of Man! Rejoice in that day, and leap for joy, for behold, your reward is great in heaven; for so their fathers did to the prophets" (Luke 6:22–23).

In the face of opposition and persecution, we must cling to the truth of God's Word and the hope of our salvation, remaining "steadfast, immovable, always abounding in the work of the Lord" (1 Corinthians 15:58).

A Spirit of Expectancy and Hope

In light of these turbulent times, we must live with a spirit of expectancy and hope, looking forward to the glorious appearing of "our great God and Savior Jesus Christ" (Titus 2:13). This blessed hope should fill us with joy, peace, and anticipation, even in the midst of trials and tribulations.

The apostle Paul, writing to the Thessalonian church, told them to "encourage one another with these words" (1 Thessalonians 4:18), reminding them of the hope they had in the return of Christ. As we witness the unfolding of prophetic events, we too must encourage one another, reminding each other of the promises of God and the certainty of His imminent return.

Our hope is not in the temporal circumstances of this world but in the eternal reality of Christ's reign and the promise of His glorious return. As the apostle Peter declared,

> But according to his promise we are waiting for new heavens and a new earth in which righteousness dwells (2 Peter 3:13).

This hope should anchor our souls and sustain us through the storms of life, for we know that our Redeemer lives, and He is coming again.

The Certainty of God's Promises

Amidst the turmoil and uncertainty of our times, we can find comfort and assurance in the certainty of God's promises. Throughout the ages, the Lord has faithfully fulfilled His Word, and He will not fail to bring to pass the ultimate triumph of His Kingdom. God's promises are eternal and unchanging, and they will be fulfilled in their appointed time.

As we witness the unfolding of prophetic events and the convergence of signs pointing to the imminence of Christ's return, we can cling to the promise of the Lord Jesus Himself:

> "Heaven and earth will pass away, but my words will not pass away" (Matthew 24:35).

The apostle Peter, writing to the believers of his day, encouraged them to "set your hope fully on the grace that will be brought to you at the revelation of Jesus Christ" (1 Peter 1:13). This grace, this unmerited favor of God, is the foundation of our faith and the source of our hope in the midst of trials and tribulations.

Faithful and Watchful

As we witness the unfolding of prophetic events and the convergence of signs pointing to the imminence of Christ's return, let us be found faithful and watchful, like the wise virgins who kept their lamps burning in anticipation of the bridegroom's return (Matthew 25:1–13). Let us cling to the promise that "he who began a good work in you will bring it to completion at the day of Jesus Christ" (Philippians 1:6).

The King is coming! Though the nations rage and the world shakes, He is on the throne and on the move. Let us be found faithful, fearless, and focused when He appears, proclaiming the hope of the gospel and pointing the lost to the only source of true peace and security—our Lord and Savior, Jesus Christ.

Appendix

Ezekiel 38 and 39

Prophecy Against Gog

38

The word of the LORD came to me: [2] "Son of man, set your face toward Gog, of the land of Magog, the chief prince of Meshech and Tubal, and prophesy against him [3] and say, Thus says the Lord GOD: Behold, I am against you, O Gog, chief prince of Meshech and Tubal. [4] And I will turn you about and put hooks into your jaws, and I will bring you out, and all your army, horses and horsemen, all of them clothed in full armor, a great host, all of them with buckler and shield, wielding swords. [5] Persia, Cush, and Put are with them, all of them with shield and helmet; [6] Gomer and all his hordes; Beth-togarmah from the uttermost parts of the north with all his hordes—many peoples are with you.

[7] "Be ready and keep ready, you and all your hosts that are assembled about you, and be a guard for them. [8] After many days you will be mustered. In the latter years you will go against the land that is restored from war, the land whose people were gathered from many

peoples upon the mountains of Israel, which had been a continual waste. Its people were brought out from the peoples and now dwell securely, all of them. [9] You will advance, coming on like a storm. You will be like a cloud covering the land, you and all your hordes, and many peoples with you.

[10] "Thus says the Lord GOD: On that day, thoughts will come into your mind, and you will devise an evil scheme [11] and say, 'I will go up against the land of unwalled villages. I will fall upon the quiet people who dwell securely, all of them dwelling without walls, and having no bars or gates,' [12] to seize spoil and carry off plunder, to turn your hand against the waste places that are now inhabited, and the people who were gathered from the nations, who have acquired livestock and goods, who dwell at the center of the earth. [13] Sheba and Dedan and the merchants of Tarshish and all its leaders will say to you, 'Have you come to seize spoil? Have you assembled your hosts to carry off plunder, to carry away silver and gold, to take away livestock and goods, to seize great spoil?'

[14] "Therefore, son of man, prophesy, and say to Gog, Thus says the Lord GOD: On that day when my people Israel are dwelling securely, will you not know it? [15] You will come from your place out of the uttermost parts of the north, you and many peoples with you, all of them riding on horses, a great host, a mighty army. [16] You will come up against my people Israel, like a cloud covering the land. In the latter days I will bring you against my land, that the nations may know me, when through you, O Gog, I vindicate my holiness before their eyes.

[17] "Thus says the Lord GOD: Are you he of whom I spoke in former days by my servants the prophets of Israel, who in those days prophesied for years that I would bring you against them? [18] But on that day, the day that Gog shall come against the land of Israel, declares the Lord GOD, my wrath will be roused in my anger. [19] For in my jealousy and in my blazing wrath I declare, On that day there shall be a great earthquake in the land of Israel. [20] The fish of the sea and the birds of the heavens and the beasts of the field and all creeping things that creep on the ground, and all the people who are on the face of the earth, shall quake at my presence. And the mountains shall be thrown down, and the cliffs shall fall, and every wall shall tumble to the ground. [21] I will summon a sword against Gog on all my mountains, declares the Lord GOD. Every man's sword will be against his brother. [22] With pestilence and bloodshed I will enter into judgment with him, and I will rain upon him and his hordes and the many peoples who are with him torrential rains and hailstones, fire and sulfur. [23] So I will show my greatness and my holiness and make myself known in the eyes of many nations. Then they will know that I am the LORD.

39

"And you, son of man, prophesy against Gog and say, Thus says the Lord GOD: Behold, I am against you, O Gog, chief prince of Meshech and Tubal. [2] And I will turn you about and drive you forward, and bring you up from the uttermost parts of the north, and lead you against the mountains of Israel. [3] Then I will strike your bow from your left hand, and will make your arrows drop out of your right hand. [4] You shall fall on the mountains of Israel, you and all your hordes and the peoples who are with you. I will give you to birds of prey of every sort and to the beasts of the field to be devoured. [5] You shall fall in the open field, for I have spoken, declares the Lord God. [6] I will send fire on Magog and on those who dwell securely in the coastlands, and they shall know that I am the Lord.

[7] "And my holy name I will make known in the midst of my people Israel, and I will not let my holy name be profaned anymore. And the nations shall know that I am the Lord, the Holy One in Israel. [8] Behold, it is coming and it will be brought about, declares the Lord God. That is the day of which I have spoken.

[9] "Then those who dwell in the cities of Israel will go out and make fires of the weapons and burn them, shields and bucklers, bow and arrows, clubs and spears; and they will make fires of them for seven years, [10] so that they will not need to take wood out of the field or cut down any out of the forests, for they will make their fires of the weapons. They will seize the spoil of those who despoiled them, and plunder those who plundered them, declares the Lord God.

[11] "On that day I will give to Gog a place for burial in Israel, the Valley of the Travelers, east of the sea. It will block the travelers, for there Gog and all his multitude will be buried. It will be called the Valley of Hamon-gog. [12] For seven months the house of Israel will be burying them, in order to cleanse the land. [13] All the people of the land will bury them, and it will

bring them renown on the day that I show my glory, declares the Lord GOD. [14] They will set apart men to travel through the land regularly and bury those travelers remaining on the face of the land, so as to cleanse it. At the end of seven months they will make their search. [15] And when these travel through the land and anyone sees a human bone, then he shall set up a sign by it, till the buriers have buried it in the Valley of Hamon-gog. [16] (Hamonah is also the name of the city.) Thus shall they cleanse the land.

[17] "As for you, son of man, thus says the Lord GOD: Speak to the birds of every sort and to all beasts of the field: 'Assemble and come, gather from all around to the sacrificial feast that I am preparing for you, a great sacrificial feast on the mountains of Israel, and you shall eat flesh and drink blood. [18] You shall eat the flesh of the mighty, and drink the blood of the princes of the earth—of rams, of lambs, and of he-goats, of bulls, all of them fat beasts of Bashan. [19] And you shall eat fat till you are filled, and drink blood till you are drunk, at the sacrificial feast that I am preparing for you. [20] And you shall be filled at my table with horses and charioteers, with mighty men and all kinds of warriors,' declares the Lord GOD.

[21] "And I will set my glory among the nations, and all the nations shall see my judgment that I have executed, and my hand that I have laid on them. [22] The house of Israel shall know that I am the LORD their God, from that day forward. [23] And the nations shall know that the house of Israel went into captivity for their iniquity, because they dealt so treacherously with me that I hid my face from them and gave them into

the hand of their adversaries, and they all fell by the sword. [24] I dealt with them according to their uncleanness and their transgressions, and hid my face from them.

The LORD Will Restore Israel

[25] "Therefore thus says the Lord GOD: Now I will restore the fortunes of Jacob and have mercy on the whole house of Israel, and I will be jealous for my holy name. [26] They shall forget their shame and all the treachery they have practiced against me, when they dwell securely in their land with none to make them afraid, [27] when I have brought them back from the peoples and gathered them from their enemies' lands, and through them have vindicated my holiness in the sight of many nations. [28] Then they shall know that I am the LORD their God, because I sent them into exile among the nations and then assembled them into their own land. I will leave none of them remaining among the nations anymore. [29] And I will not hide my face anymore from them, when I pour out my Spirit upon the house of Israel, declares the Lord GOD."

Scripture Index